outdoor tips

L. W. "Bill" Johnson, "The Hunter"
Robert Elman   Jerry Gibbs

A Benjamin Company/Rutledge Book

Cover photo: Marti Felbinger
Artwork: Richard Amundsen
ISBN O-87502-905-1
Copyright © 1972 by Remington Arms Company, Inc.
Prepared and produced by Rutledge Books, Inc., and The Benjamin Company, Inc.
All rights reserved under International and Pan-American Convention
Published by The Benjamin Company, Inc.
485 Madison Avenue, New York, New York 10022
Library of Congress Catalog Card Number 76-121738
Printed in the United States of America

Contents

About the authors

L. W. "Bill" Johnson is called "The Hunter," and he has earned the name and the reputation. Bill Johnson has hunted just about every game bird and animal that lives within the United States. For many years, Bill Johnson has conducted a weekly television program on WSAU-TV in Wausau, Wisconsin. The program, "The Hunter," is syndicated in various cities throughout the United States, and from it thousands of viewers have been able to gather hunting information, hints and suggestions that Bill has spent a lifetime accumulating. He is an expert in the field. His first book, the *Wild Game Cookbook,* has become a classic in the few years since its publication. As was the case with the cookbook, many of the tips here were gathered in response to a contest sponsored by Bill's television program.

Robert Elman, formerly editor of *The American Sportsman* quarterly, is now a free-lance writer specializing in outdoor recreation. He has edited a number of manuals on outdoor skills, including *Vacation Fishing* and *Camping Skills, Places, Pleasures.* Among the books he has written is one for youngsters, entitled *Discover the Outdoors.* Bob is presently writing a book on the subject of hiking. His most recently published book, coauthored by arms historian Harold L. Peterson, is *The Great Guns.* Another of his volumes, *The American Shooting Prints,* is now on press.

Jerry Gibbs is currently assistant outdoors editor of *True* magazine and *True*'s yearbooks on hunting and fishing. For some years he edited *Camping Journal,* a monthly devoted to family outdoor recreation. He has hunted, fished or camped over much of North America and the Caribbean area. His stories and photographs on outdoor subjects have appeared in such major national magazines as *Field & Stream, Outdoor Life, Sports Afield,* as well as many others. Jerry has been an active outdoorsman since boyhood, losing only three years of sport during a stint with the U.S. Navy.

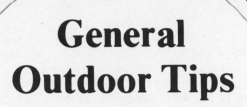

General
Outdoor Tips

There are many skills, bits of knowledge, tricks and procedures that, when learned, will increase the fun, comfort and safety of any outing whether it be hiking, shooting, fishing, camping, hunting or touring with a recreational vehicle.

■ Anyone who spends much time outdoors should learn to forecast weather. Cloud formations and color are the most reliable natural forecasters, and it will cost you only a quarter to learn about them. Send your money, with a request for the booklet entitled *Clouds,* to the Superintendent of Documents, U.S. Government Printing Office, Washington, D.C., 20402. After a little practice at matching the illustrations in the book with the clouds in the sky you'll be able to judge with fair accuracy what weather tomorrow will bring. Bear in mind that if rain starts quickly after the clouds gather, a storm is likely to be short; a long cloud buildup usually means a long rain.

■ There was a time when outdoorsmen associated dogs with hunting and not much else, but people now seem to take their pets along just for company. Regardless of the season, every dog should have his day—a bit of shade, a dish full of cool (not ice-cold) fresh water and a chance to romp when evening comes.

■ Although one can hardly blame biting insects for preferring women to men, the ladies are understandably reluctant to accept these advances. Sometimes even insect repellent fails to discourage determined biters, but a girl can make herself less attractive to annoying insects by going without hair spray and cosmetics, the odors of which seem to attract the pests.

■ Take gloves and a head net on any trip into the North Country. If you run into a plague of blackflies, you may find them both murderous and immune to repellent. A smudge fire will discourage them to some degree, but while you're moving about, you'll want to have every inch of skin covered.

■ Topographic maps are invaluable guides to have when you're going through unfamiliar regions. Nearly every square mile of the United States has been mapped by the Geological Survey, and detailed contour maps are available. Whichever ones you need will be listed in an index by state. For a free index of any state west of the Mississippi River, write to the Denver Distribution Center, Geological Survey, Federal Center, Denver, Colorado,

80225. East of the Mississippi, write to the Washington Distribution Center, Geological Survey, Washington, D.C., 20242. You can then order the desired "quadrangle" from the same source for the nominal charge listed in the index. Trail maps are also available. For areas in the eastern United States, write to the Appalachian Trail Conference, 1718 N Street, NW, Washington, D.C., 20036. For western trail maps, write to the Sierra Club, 1050 Mills Tower, San Francisco, California, 94104. When you have received your maps, back them with pieces of cloth bonded on with wallpaper paste. Pocket-carried paper maps are unfolded and refolded so many times that they may fall apart unless they are properly reinforced.

■ Your watch can serve as an emergency compass. To use it, point the hour hand toward the sun. South will lie in the middle of the angle formed by the hour hand and the numeral *12* on the watch face, and north will be at the point opposite it.

■ Telephone lines and power lines can serve as guidelines in remote areas. The poles and high-tension towers are usually marked with consecutive numbers, giving you reference markers and a trail back toward camp, road, settlement or other access point. If you're lost, following power lines will eventually lead you back to civilization.

■ On your map, mark the point where you take off into any unsettled area. Then mark your destination and draw a line from start to goal. Check the direction with the compass that you, naturally, have with you. Notice landmarks (peaks, valleys, tall trees, rock formations, waters) lying in the desired direction and follow the trail they make. Then check yourself via compass and map once in a while as you line up new landmarks.

■ If you get lost, sit and rest for a few minutes; people can often find their way again after allowing themselves a time to rest and calm down. If you still can't figure out your location, climb a tree and look for landmarks. Generally, the shortest way out is toward any road, smoke, building or other sign of civilization you spot. Waterways also lead toward settlements. Follow them downstream.

■ Being able to maintain contact with one another during an outing is important, especially when children are along. Each member should be equipped with a police-type whistle for this purpose and be instructed to follow a previously set-up signal code. Traditionally, three short blasts—just like three gunshots or three smudge fires—mean "Help!" or "I'm lost." You can work out other signals for "Chow's on," "Time to get out of the water," etc. Whistle power carries farther and is less tiring than lung power.

■ Reflector tape is great for marking things around camp so that you can find them easily in the dark. When you explore an area, use it to mark trees to guide you back to camp either before or after dark.

■ Many commercial campgrounds maintain bulletin boards for messages and have telephones for those who want to call home. Before leaving on a trip, try to let relatives and friends know where and when you plan to stop. If you wish to receive mail along the way, tell them when you plan to pass through various towns. They can send letters or packages to you in care of General Delivery at any post office. Anything mailed far enough ahead of time will be waiting to be picked up when you get there.

■ Boots for winter wear, including insulated boots, should be larger than your usual shoe size. If they don't feel a trifle large when you try them on, go up a half size. The extra space lets you wear two pairs of socks for insulation, absorption and padding. The inner pair may be lighter and thinner than the outer pair, but the best material for both is cotton or wool—never one of the nonabsorbent synthetics.

■ When lacing your boots, tie a square knot at the instep and then finish lacing up the ankle and calf. In this way you can make the foot section tight enough for good support and still keep the upper portion comfortably loose. To remove odors from boots, dust the insides with powdered borax.

■ Don't dry boots with strong heat, as this will make them hard and brittle, perhaps even causing cracks. Commercial boot driers are great for home use. Or you can stuff the boots with newspapers and let them dry naturally. You can speed up the process by inserting a *small* light bulb on an extension cord into each boot, or you can reverse a vacuum cleaner's flow and blow warm air into them. A ladies' hair drier is even more efficient for the purpose. In camp, you can put hand warmers into them or fill them with fire-warmed pebbles. Hang hip boots or waders upside down to drain by hooking the feet into an ordinary clothes hanger. Incidentally, the tops of worn-out hip boots can serve as waterproof leggings.

■ Boot laces rubbed with beeswax or paraffin are less apt to catch burrs and briers and to come untied than untreated ones.

■ Before turning in at night, replace one of the fireplace rocks with a covered metal bucket or ten-gallon milk can full of water. Though the fire dies, the container will hold enough heat to give you warm water in the morning.

■ When the felt soles on hip boots or waders wear out, replace them with scrap outdoor carpeting. Glued on with waterproof cement, it will provide as much traction as felt, will outlast it and will absorb far less water.

■ You can improvise a wilderness washbasin by digging a shal-

9

low hole in the ground and lining it with a plastic ground cloth. This beats fussing with a bulky, hard-to-pack metal basin.

■ Mesquite beans are a good desert-survival food. Chew the pods and beans together to get all the juices. Swallow the whole works if you can; if not, discard them and chew some more. You can also boil the beans and pods in water. After the water cools, drink it. It may then be easier to eat the beans and pods, too, since cooking softens them a bit.

■ In a hot climate, ignore the old wives' tale that says you should eat only light, salad-type meals. Eat normal amounts and stick to high-protein foods. Avoid food and drink with high sugar contents. Don't drink alcoholic beverages during the daytime. Wear loose-fitting clothing and fishnet underwear. Drink plenty of water. If you must drink ice water, take it very slowly. Engage in light exercise and sport—sweating is good for you. Pack salt tablets but remember that they should be taken very sparingly. Follow the recommendations on the label.

■ Indians often burned dried bearberries and wild aster roots in their fires to attract deer. Similarly, many wildlife photographers have found that burning incense will attract inquisitive deer and other animals.

■ If an animal becomes mesmerized by your car's headlights, slow down immediately and blink your lamps—high beams to low beams or even off and on again. This will get the animal moving, but watch carefully as you proceed, as there may be more animals ready to cross the road.

■ A good hiking staff can be made from a dry sapling pole about five feet long and an inch thick, plus a spike, some thin wire and a

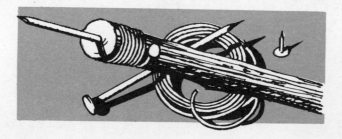

short tack or screw. Wind the wire around the bottom inch of the thicker end of the pole. Then wind the end of the wire around the tack or screw, and drive it all the way into the wood. A secure wire wrapping will reinforce the end of the staff. Cut off the head of the spike with a file or hacksaw, sharpen it and hammer it into the wired end of the staff so that the point protrudes.

■ A toilet-tissue holder can be made from a two-pound coffee can by punching two holes in it opposite each other and near the bottom. Run some line through the holes, and tie the can to a tree or

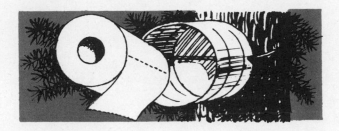

stake at the latrine. The can will keep the paper dry in any weather but a driving rain, and you can put the plastic lid on it for extra protection.

■ A plastic ground cloth can serve as an emergency water bucket. Just tie two opposite corners together. When the rig is dipped into a stream or lake, the untied corners will bend up as water fills the center. Carry it by the knot as you would a basket. A four-foot-square sheet will hold a couple of gallons.

■ A heater is invaluable equipment to have if your vehicle should become stranded during cold weather. Emergency heaters can be made from a couple of one- or two-pound coffee cans with plastic lids. Carry several plumber's candles in each can along with a supply of matches. Melt some wax in the bottom of each can and hold the candles upright in the wax pools until they have hardened. When the candles have been lighted, they will generate a surprising amount of comforting warmth.

■ Asphalt shingles can help move a vehicle stuck in the snow. Place them snugly in front of the wheels, rough side down, and drive over them slowly.

■ Carry an extra pair of wool socks in your car, boat or hunting coat. A change of socks at midday will make you feel fresh and ready to go again.

■ Sawdust mixed with kerosene is a sure fire-starter. In a tightly sealed can, it can be stowed in your car or truck.

■ The uses of empty plastic bleach jugs are probably limited by only the human imagination. Some of them are mentioned in other sections. In addition to those: Poke holes in a plastic jug, and you will have a chum pot that will attract fish for long periods—just fill it with chum and hang it over the side of the boat. Or paint a jug and make it into a duck decoy. Tightly capped, an empty gallon jug will keep an adult afloat in the event of accident.

■ An angel-food cake pan makes an untippable drinking bowl for a dog when you drive a wooden stake through the pan's center hole into the ground.

■ Insect repellent (perhaps the greatest achievement of the age for outdoor living) will usually ward off ticks as well as other bugs. Although it works on pets as well as on people, it should be used sparingly on animals as they may lick it.

■ A cool summer doghouse can be constructed from a fifty-gallon oil drum. Cut one end out, add bedding, find a shady spot for it and set it on blocks to keep rainwater from running in.

■ Winter campers, ice fishermen and hunters can all get in trouble on thin ice. Check it before venturing onto an unknown expanse. If you must walk across strange ice, cut a pole and carry it as if you were a tightrope walker. The pole will prevent you from going all the way in if the ice should crack.

■ Commercial waterproof matches show up occasionally in camping-goods stores, but it's easy to make your own. The best matches for outdoor use are the wooden kind that will light when struck on any rough surface. To waterproof them, coat the heads with nail polish or melted paraffin. Large matches are recommended. When used to light a fire, the match itself becomes part of the tinder and should be long enough to burn for a few moments.

■ As protective match cases, some people use cylindrical plastic pill containers; others use the small metal cans in which color film is packaged (though the thirty-five-millimeter size will hold only short matches). Still others prefer an empty plastic shotgun shell stopped with a waxed cork to keep moisture out. Two empty shells, one 12 gauge and one 20 gauge, will fit snugly together to make still another type of match case.

■ It has been mentioned that you're safe from lightning inside your car. You're *not* safe under most trees. Beech trees, however, are rarely hit, so if you're caught in the woods and there are beeches nearby, you're better off under them than under other trees. Rain usually means good fishing, but in the event of a real storm—with or without lightning—play it safe and get to shore fast.

■ In cold rain or spray, thinly applied petroleum jelly (Vaseline) will protect your face from chapping just as lip balm will keep your lips from cracking. There are also balms available for hands. When it's not cold enough to wear conventional gloves, some people wear rubber dishwashing gloves or skin-diving gloves to protect sensitive skin from spray.

■ Emergency torches can be made from tightly rolled newspapers by soaking one end of the roll in paraffin. When using them, however, take care not to get burned or start a fire as the flame eats its way down. This type of torch also makes a fine fire-starter. Your kids will much prefer emergency torches made from cattails though. Just soak the head in kerosene and light it. There's something mysterious and adventurous-feeling about a natural torch. It gives kids the same tingle as a campfire after dark.

■ You don't have to be a pipe smoker to love fuzzy pipe cleaners. When the little green inchworms are around in May, June and July, green pipe cleaners, cut into short lengths and wrapped around small trout hooks, are fine homemade flies. If you can't find green ones, dip white ones in vegetable dye. On rainy days, they can also furnish amusement for youngsters confined to camp or camper. They can twist them into dolls, doll furniture, animal shapes and so on. A pipe cleaner can also be twisted around the neck of a bag to keep it closed—other uses will occur to you as the need arises.

■ Another handy item to have is a small square of the self-sticking paper used to cover kitchen shelves. Since it will stick well to almost any dry surface—even a tent or rain parka—you can use it for temporary repair of many fabrics.

■ If you don't bother a skunk, he usually won't bother you, so if one comes prowling, attracted by the smell of food, leave the visitor to his own devices. If, however, you inadvertently frighten him into turning those devices on you, the best treatment is to scrub with carbolic soap and water. In severe cases, wash the skin with gasoline. Wash your eyes with water or a mild boric-acid or other ophthalmic solution. Cleaning the scalp is the toughest problem; if the aftereffects linger, an unfashionably short haircut may be necessary. The odor can usually be removed from clothing by a six-hour soak in tomato juice, or you can wash the clothing in ammonia or chloride of lime, then rinse it well and hang it in the breeze. Tomato juice is fairly effective on people and dogs as well as on clothing. Except in bad cases, a generous application, vigorously rubbed into hair and skin, will kill the odor.

■ Always air a sleeping bag after it's been dry-cleaned. Carbon tetrachloride, used in some cleaning agents, can be fatal if inhaled over a long period of time. Some cleaners use agents that are harmless both to the materials of the bag and to human beings, so you might ask for them when you bring your bag in. And some of the latest sleeping bags, though water-repellent and insulated, are washable.

■ The only poisonous reptiles in this country are the rattler, cottonmouth (water moccasin), copperhead and coral snake, plus the Southwest's gila monster, sometimes called the beaded lizard. The Southwest also is the region of poisonous scorpions. Several spiders can inflict painful bites, but only two—the black widow and the brown recluse—are seriously venomous. You should read about each of these species in a field guide and know whether it inhabits the area where you pursue your outdoor activities. If so, wear snakeproof boots and memorize the appearance of the species so that you won't approach it with the impression that it's harmless. But don't let such worries spoil an outing. When normal precautions are taken, venomous bites or stings are rare—and fatalities exceedingly rare. You should, of course, have a snakebite kit, which includes a tourniquet (applied above the punctures to stop the flow of venom through the circulatory system), a sharp, sterile blade to make incisions across the punctures to facilitate withdrawal of the venom, a suction cup which is used to draw out the poison and an antiseptic. Spider bites and scorpion stings can be treated like snakebites. After first aid, get to a doctor as quickly as possible, but don't speed up circulation by overexerting yourself.

■ In addition to the pests mentioned above, even a bee or wasp can be dangerous to someone who is allergic to its sting and has not had preventive treatment. If you suspect that someone in your family has such an allergy, check with your doctor before your next outdoor excursion.

■ Before trying to dig out a bad splinter, chill the skin around it with an ice pack or piece of ice. This minor local anesthetic is especially helpful when the splinter victim is a youngster and each whimper hurts you worse than the heat-sterilized needle hurts the child.

■ A time *not* to apply cold is when your skin is frostbitten. Rubbing snow on frostbite is a terrible mistake. Don't massage the whitened area, either, but do encourage circulation by exercising. And apply warmth (not excessive heat). Even cupping your hand over it will help. Better yet, wet a handkerchief with moderately hot water and apply it gently to warm the frostbitten area.

■ Everyone agrees that a first-aid kit is essential, yet too few people pack one. Necessary items (aside from the previously mentioned snakebite kit for snake-infested areas) include antiseptic, adhesive bandage strips, squares or a roll of gauze bandage, elastic bandage, tape, scissors, tweezers, a tourniquet and aspirin. No need to list a needle for removing splinters because you have needles in the very essential emergency sewing kit which you didn't forget to pack. You may also want to have a balm for stings and burns, calamine lotion or a similar preparation, needle-nosed pliers with a wire-cutting edge—not just for porcupine-quill removal, for which you might prefer a hemostat, but for removing a fishhook from a person—plus sunburn lotion, ophthalmic ointment, water-purifying tablets (or a purification kit) and something to remedy indigestion.

■ Ordinary mouthwash or witch hazel will soothe insect bites. Still better for bites, stings and even poison-ivy itch is a paste made with water and baking soda (which is well to have along for cooking, anyway). Baking soda can also be dissolved in water and drunk to treat an upset stomach or left in solution and added to pots, utensils, vacuum bottles and insulated coolers to remove odors.

15

Camping
and
Hiking

Almost every outdoor activity proves to be simpler, easier, less fatiguing and more fun than someone who hasn't tried it thinks. That is, it's all those things to the person who is properly clothed and equipped and who knows the tricks and techniques for getting the most out of an excursion away from the modern urban bustle into nature's more serene realm.

Hiking is a perfect example of a pastime that's much less demanding than many people realize.

Though a forced march over twenty (or even five) miles would be enervating, especially with a heavy pack, an equally long ramble through the countryside can be invigorating fun. The secrets of making it really enjoyable include having proper clothing and equipment, a proper pack (when a pack is needed), a proper walking technique (which is easy to master, but involves more than just planting one foot ahead of the other), a comfortable pace, an interest in the surroundings and sufficiently frequent stops for resting, eating and enjoying other activities. For the most part, the same rules apply to camping. The most important tip we can offer is to *pack this book along on your next outing.* Then, if you encounter a camping problem or can't quite remember the best approach to some camping activity, you can look up the answer.

■ Elsewhere in this book, tips are offered on specialized clothing and equipment for specialized kinds of recreation, such as winter camping, rec-vehicle camping, snowmobiling, etc., but generally speaking, what works well for ordinary hiking works well for most kinds of camping. Footwear is a prime example. Never hike or camp wearing shoes or boots that haven't been broken in thoroughly enough to be soft and pliable. Even the best hiking boots can torture you if they haven't been softened and somewhat formed to your feet. This can be done by wearing them for several days around home or camp or on a number of short walks before really taking to the trail. Rubbing them with neat's-foot oil or saddle soap will also help to make the leather supple.

■ For short hikes, a rugged pair of everyday walking shoes will do, as will canvas sneakers or tennis shoes with cleated rubber soles. Even hard-soled moccasins are all right, but the soft-soled type can cause blisters if used for anything but snowshoeing, lounging around camp or boating. For longer hikes and all-around hiking and camping, you should have pliable but firm leather boots that are high enough to provide ankle support. The most suitable all-purpose boots have tops that vary from five inches to a little more than eight inches in height. Although some old-timers still prefer leather heels and soles, the consensus is definitely in favor of thick, lugged heels and soles made of durable rubber or—best of all—a composite, which offers both comfort and traction. Whether the exterior is rough- or smooth-finished, the interior should be smooth. Steel shanks, toe reinforcements and padded tongues and ankles are refinements found on very good models. This padding is not necessarily insulation. Winter-insulated boots are a blessing in cold weather, but if used in summer, they can be too hot and become clammy from perspiration. Boots should be snug at the heel but roomy inside (in both width and length), especially toward the toe. Besides needing to allow space for two pairs of socks, you must leave room for your feet to expand, which they will do on a long walk or under the weight of a pack.

■ On long hikes or extended camping trips, pack an extra pair of shoes or boots—not only because you may need them in an emergency but because switching footwear will rest your feet.

■ Mesh insoles provide cushioning, let air circulate and help to keep your feet dry. If you buy boots and insoles separately, make sure the boots are roomy enough that the addition won't make them tight.

■ Blisters result from friction caused by the foot's rubbing against the shoe. This is usually greatest at the back of the heel and sometimes on the ball of the foot. A light sprinkling of talcum powder —a good item to pack on a camping trip—will help prevent them. Even more effective is a little moist soap rubbed on the backs of your heels; then dust your socks with talcum or foot powder. Also be sure to have adhesive bandages with you. If a tender spot develops, cover it right away with an adhesive bandage to absorb friction.

■ When you stop for a rest by a stream or creek, cool your body rapidly by wetting your wrists. It will also be a great joy to remove boots and socks and soak your feet—but be sure to dry them thoroughly afterward. It is also a good idea at that point to put on clean socks. However, if your feet have become swollen, do not remove your boots unless you plan to stay there quite awhile or are certain you can get the boots on again. A sufficiently long soaking will relieve swelling, as will, to some extent, loosening boot laces enough to be comfortable.

■ On short easy hikes or around camp, short pants are comfortable in warm weather, but only long pants are practical in changeable weather or for hiking over rough terrain, climbing, pushing through scratchy brush, etc. They will even provide some protection from sunburn, scratches and insect bites. If you wear jeans, avoid the tight "cowboy" style—they must be roomy or you'll be uncomfortable on a long hike. Loose slacks made of closely woven chino, denim, drill, poplin or a similar material are fine. To avoid snagging, they should be cuffless. For mountain hiking, they should be warm and sturdy regardless of the time of year. For traveling through brushy woods or cactus-choked stretches, hunter's brush pants are ideal because of their reinforced protective facings; however, they may be too warm and heavy for general hiking.

■ The belt you choose to wear should be soft, comfortable, moderately wide and strong, since it may have to hold up a canteen and a folding or sheath knife as well as your pants. Beltless slacks are a poor idea for hiking and camping because they have no loops to act as equipment hangers.

■ Mesh or quilted thermal underwear is great in the winter. Very light or mesh underwear is also great in the summer because it actually serves as cooling insulation and absorbs moisture. The wash-and-wear kind is best.

■ When choosing your outdoor shirts, remember that whereas long sleeves can be rolled up, short sleeves can't be rolled down. You should also pack a sweater, a short windbreaker with big pockets, a brimmed or billed hat (for protection from rain as well as sun), a poncho or hooded rain jacket and sunglasses (even in winter, and preferably Polaroid).

■ Food suggestions for camping trips are included in the cooking section, but it must be added here that snacks should be carried on hikes of even moderate duration. You'll need the energy they provide. Good snacks for refueling without adding much bulk or weight to your pack include fresh and dried fruits, candy, nuts, hardtack, crackers, dried or freeze-dried mixes, cheese, smoked meats and small sandwiches. You might also want a vacuum bottle of something hot or cold to drink, depending on the season— fruit juice, coffee, tea or a hearty soup. Carbonated drinks are not recommended when you're exerting yourself. Milk is all right for short hikes but doesn't keep very well.

■ Carry a full canteen, and be sure that the water you use to re-fill it is clean. If you have the slightest doubt that the water is pure, boil it for ten minutes. This will make it taste flat, but you can make it taste good again by letting it cool and then pouring it from one container to another several times. Or you can simply add a little lemon or lime juice (or powder). If you have no time to boil it, treat it with water-purifying tablets, such as halazone, or use a chemical purifying and filtering kit. These are available at camping-supply stores. Many campers prefer to take no chances: They boil their water and then purify it, too.

■ Don't drink too much of any liquid or too fast. In very hot climates take salt tablets with your water. Also remember that thirst can be temporarily quenched by sucking on a piece of orange or lemon—or a clean pebble.

■ Other items that add to fun (or convenience) on even short hikes are a folding pocketknife (carried most comfortably on a belt clip), a camera, binoculars, a compass, a map (varnished or oiled and re-inforced to make it waterproof and durable), sunburn lotion, insect repellent, a first-aid kit, paper tissues and towels, waterproof matches, disposable towelettes and pocket-sized illustrated field guides to whatever most interests you—birds, animals, trees, wild flowers, insects, etc.

■ Your expedition's junior members can carry their share of the supplies in small, light rucksacks. If a rucksack isn't overloaded and has adjustable straps, it will be quite comfortable. Most children are eager to wear one because it makes them feel adventurous and grown-up. For long hikes (and for storing gear at camp), the teen-agers and adults will need larger backpacks. A fairly big, flexible "mountain-climber's" rucksack will do for carrying moderate amounts of gear. Roomier and more comfortable is the open-topped Adirondack pack basket, made of woven ash or willow strips and worn, like a rucksack, with adjustable shoulder straps. Even roomier, more comfortable still and most versatile is the Everest-style tubular aluminum pack frame and detachable pack. This style is the best by far for more ambitious hikes or camp-outs. Contoured so that the metal frame won't dig into you, the weight is supported by adjustable padded shoulder straps and by flexible web straps against the back. (To ease the weight of heavy loads, buy a detachable, padded hip belt that hooks on at the bottom.) The frame bottom turns rearward in a flat or modified L-shaped shelf so that no equipment will slip down. A sleeping bag (perhaps with a few camp items stowed inside it) can be rolled tightly and lashed at the bottom of the frame, with the pack slipped onto the frame above it and/or with other gear lashed on above.

■ When loading a pack, put the heaviest items at the top. You'll be more comfortable with the weight up near your shoulders than with it lower on your back. But don't overdo this trick, as a very top-heavy pack will unbalance you and make walking difficult. Hard-edged items should be packed so that they don't touch your back or shoulders. Items that will be needed soon or frequently should be stowed in the pack's exterior pockets. There are conflicting opinions about optimum total weight, but the general rule is to go light whenever possible. The most an adult should attempt to carry on an all-day trek (even with plenty of time out for lunch and rests) is probably thirty pounds. A youngster should carry less than half that much. The more people who join the outing, the less each one will have to carry.

■ For resting, the best position to assume is on the back, with the feet propped up against a tree or on a log or rock.

■ If the shoulder straps of your pack begin to chafe, pad underneath them with a small towel. On long treks, you can further ease the burden of a heavy load by attaching a tumpline—a strap that slings across the forehead—to your pack so that your neck muscles can do some of the work.

■ Sleeping bags come in many sizes and models, but they all fall into one of two general types: the rectangular and the mummy. The mummy bag is form-fitting with an adjustable hood designed for head warmth. Expensive ones are insulated with pure goose down. Although goose down provides the greatest warmth and the least weight, Dacron and other insulating materials are adequate for most camping. The very warm but lightweight mummy bag is popular in cold climates, but it is somewhat confining. The more-popular rectangular type is roomier, easier to roll and best for all-around camping. It employs the same types of insulation and will often have a detachable liner of flannel or some other material for accommodation to temperature changes. It will also usually have a top flap that can be propped up like an awning to protect your head from wind or rain, though this is hardly necessary when it's used in a tent. Regardless of the style of your sleeping bag, it should have an outer material that is water-repellent, *not* waterproof. It has to "breathe" or it will become damp inside. Some bags have rubberized bottoms to keep out ground moisture, but these hinder dry cleaning. A ground cloth, air mattress or waterproof-floored tent is better for this purpose. And a rustproof, heavy-duty zipper makes a much better closure than snap-fasteners make.

■ In cold weather, a sweat suit makes a great set of camping pajamas; in mild weather, you will need nothing more than lightweight, clean underwear if your sleeping bag is well insulated.

■ Like sleeping bags, tents should be water-repellent, not waterproof, except for the built-in ground cloth, or flooring, featured in many good modern tents. A tent, too, must breathe, and it won't leak if it's reasonably taut and has no rips. Before a tent is used for camping, it should be set up, wet with a garden hose and allowed to dry thoroughly. Each tent sets up differently. It may be exasperating the first time, especially if the maker's instructions aren't perfectly clear, but after that first time it will never again take more than a few minutes. The wetting down will shrink the material (so slightly that you won't notice it). After that, it won't shrink again and it won't develop water-holding sags. If put up properly, it should then be rainproof.

■ Tents and other gear can be rented from some camping-gear outlets. This is a good idea for infrequent campers and for tyros who would like to try out various equipment before deciding which models to buy.

■ If you plan to tent on loose sand or deep snow, a few pie tins with rope holes punched in their centers will be better anchors than conventional tent stakes. Run the guy rope through the tin and knot the end to prevent it from slipping out. Dig a hole for the tin, far enough from the tent and deep enough in the snow or sand to keep the rope taut and the tent upright. Then just bury it by piling on a foot or two of sand or packed snow.

■ A tent camper's sewing kit should include heavy waxed thread and a needle for canvas or a heavy-duty darning needle. Small tent rips should be repaired promptly or they'll get larger.

■ One thing that should *not* be darned is the foot section of a sock to be used for long walks, hiking or hunting. The lump resulting from such a repair is likely to cause soreness or a blister.

■ The best place to pitch camp is on level, reasonably clear ground that has good drainage and nearby supplies of water and fallen wood. High promontories are much too windy, and low valleys are likely to be flooded in a heavy rain. (For the same reason, avoid choosing a spot that is *too* near the water.)

■ As a general rule, a tent that faces southeast is well positioned for getting the morning sun and the afternoon shade. It is also protected from strong winds. In hot weather, locate it so that it will catch the breeze yet be in the shade most or all of the time. In cold weather, face it away from prevailing winds; the best positioning is with its rear to a hill or protective woods.

■ A common garden trowel is a handy camp tool. Among performing other jobs, it can be used to dig a six-inch-deep drainage ditch around your tent. This takes only a little time and will help keep you dry if the weather is wet, if the ground is not ideal for drainage or if your ground cloth is less than perfect.

■ Protecting fragile eggshells is a problem on any camping trip, but less so on packhorse outings. In the oats you pack for the horses, pack the eggs, spacing them well throughout. You'll save space and probably never break an egg.

■ Fragments of eggshell dumped into an old-fashioned camp coffeepot will make the grounds sink to the bottom more quickly and completely without affecting the taste at all.

■ An inner tube cut into inch-thick circles will give you splendid heavy-duty rubber bands that have a multiplicity of uses. Besides holding boxes together, they can be used as expansion links with the guy ropes for a tent. When stretched around a folded camp stove, they will cushion it and prevent it from knocking open.

■ Although a dry bar of soap can be stowed almost anywhere, try putting it inside your sleeping bag, particularly if it is pine- or balsam-scented. It will prevent musty odors, and when you open the outfit, you'll have your soap right there for washing.

■ An empty coffee can has many uses. When you turn it on its side and set a thick candle inside, it's a hurricane lamp. Set upright, it's a small water bucket or bait pail. It makes a good bailer. With the metal ends removed and a plastic lid put on each end, it can be painted to make a toy drum for the children around the camp. With only one end cut out, it can be painted and used as a camp flower vase or pot. With one end cut out and the plastic lid put back on, it's a waterproof holder for toilet-tissue or a spill-proof container for small utensils, gadgets or children's toys. And with the cylinder itself cut open and flattened, it's fine for a temporary reflector oven.

■ For a change from ice water, freeze lemonade, orangeade, fruit juice or a soft-drink mix in a milk carton or a plastic pitcher or jug for stowing in the luncheon cooler. It will keep the food just as cool as ordinary ice, and it will furnish a liquid treat when it begins to melt. If you chop off a few hunks when it's reached just the right melting stage, the youngsters will have sherbet.

■ One of the first rules of camp safety is to hang light-colored objects or reflector tape from every single line—tent ropes, clothes-lines, everything—that is left up at night. A line that's strung high in the dark can break a neck, and a low-strung line can trip someone. Some campers fear this possibility so strongly that they always take down a line not in use.

■ Another safety rule is to make sure there are never any food odors on your bedroll or sleeping clothes. A bear or skunk raid on the larder is to be preferred to a raid on you. For the same reason, the kitchen and the sleeping area should be separated, and food should be kept in sealed containers.

■ Safety precautions are also important with regard to fire building. First, there is never a need to build a fire right next to a tent. If your insulated sleeping bag and the shelter of the tent itself don't provide sufficient warmth, locate the fireplace far enough away to avoid the danger of sparks and put up a metal or foil reflector to direct the warmth toward you. Second, clear the fireplace area of twigs, leaves, forest humus and dry grasses; the clearing should be at least six feet wide. Third, keep your fire small. A low fire is best for most kinds of cooking, and it will give sufficient warmth if you use reflectors and build a fireplace of flat, heat-retaining and re-flecting rocks (perfectly dry ones so that there's no danger of their cracking or exploding). Fourth, keep a shovel or scoop and a bucket of water by the fireplace for drowning and burying the fire. And fifth, do drown and bury it before leaving a campsite.

■ If the fire is to provide just warmth and light, the simplest and best type to build is a tepee, or inverted-V, structure, made by loosely piling sticks over the kindling in a tepee shape. The apex will soon collapse, which is fine. You now have a star shape, hottest in the center. Push the pieces inward as they burn away and add more until it's going well. Then you can get along with the hot, slow-burning charcoal embers that remain.

■ A variation on the tepee fire is sometimes called a "dingle-stick" fire. It can be quickly built against rocks or the back of a fireplace, piled up like half a tepee. Two slightly larger logs are often placed at the sides, in a V shape, to contain it. A single skillet can be placed across the V for cooking a quick meal. Or you can dangle a couple of pots over it, on long sticks propped at an angle over it and anchored by rocks or logs.

■ The easiest-starting, hottest, fastest-burning woods are the conifers, but they are smoky and sometimes pop. Their use is really limited to getting the fire going. After that, try to use hardwoods exclusively or primarily. They'll give you a longer-lasting, less smoky fire, with better embers for both warmth and cooking and no unwanted flavors imparted to food.

■ Rolls of newspaper that have been saturated with paraffin have already been mentioned as being good fire-starters, but newspaper treated in a different way can be added to the paraffin-coated logs for a longer-burning fire when wood is scarce or wet. Saturate the paper in water, roll it into tight logs held by twine and let it dry thoroughly. Unlike ordinary paper, it will then burn quite slowly and steadily.

■ Another variation on the tepee fire is produced by adding a

25

structure to an already burning tepee fire. To build it, crisscross sticks around the rim like the walls of a log cabin, decreasing its diameter as it gets higher so that it won't tumble outward. This will give you a fast, easy, rather hot fire that will quickly form embers in the center, and it will have a fairly level top on which you can set a pot or kettle to boil water.

■ For real cooking, the best contrivance (apart from a camp stove) is a trapper fire—sometimes called a hunter-trapper fire. For this you need at least two good-sized "fire dogs"—logs that will burn slowly or not at all—or dry, flat-topped rocks. Place them in a semi-V shape, close enough together at one end to set small pots or pans across them and wide enough apart at the other end for your largest skillet. Then using any of the techniques described above, build your fire between them. If you have a grill to support the cooking ware, you can place the fire dogs parallel, instead of in a V shape, and wider apart for greater convenience.

■ Near the fireplace, drive two poles into the ground and stretch an empty clip-type fish stringer between them. The camp cook now has a handy clip line for hanging pots and pans.

Winter Camping

More Americans each year are participating in such winter sports as downhill skiing, cross-country skiing, snowshoeing, old-fashioned sleigh riding, ice skating and just plain hiking in cold but sunny weather. Since the advent of the recreational vehicle, the scope of winter sport has been greatly extended. Many people use trailer or camper vehicles as mobile winter chalets, stopping over wherever nightfall finds them.

But what about *real* camping, with tents set up right out in the snow? There's the real adventure. And you don't have to have the constitution of an Arctic explorer to do it. Space-age materials have made it possible for the average healthy person to "car camp" or backpack in the dead of winter comfortably and enjoyably.

■ Contrary to popular belief, cotton thermal knit or fishnet underwear is far from satisfactory for true winter camping. When cotton absorbs moisture, it stays clammy. The warmest underwear, worn right next to the skin, is all wool. It will take you awhile to get used to the itch, but that's a small price to pay for warmth. Next in warmness is wool underwear with a cotton or synthetic layer next to the skin. Third is synthetic material (such as nylon) or real silk. Then come the cotton thermal long johns. Fishnet underwear is good in deep-freeze conditions *over* the next-to-skin underwear, to provide dead-air space between the layers of garments.

■ If you want the ultimate in wind-retarding, insulating material in clothing, choose down. You can get it in a set of undergarments—pants and shirt—to be worn over the underwear. Or you can get it in a heavier overjacket or parka. Read the label or tag to make sure you are getting pure, prime-quality northern goose down.

■ Two types of headgear must be considered for winter camping. First is the wool stocking cap or, better, a balaclava that not only rolls down to cover ears but turns into a full face mask as well. The other type is a full hood. The hood is used under only the most severe conditions to keep all wind from ears and neck.

■ Hide, down-and-nylon insulation, fur, canvas and leather are the materials from which the warmest hand coverings—mittens—are constructed. Inside the mittens, you wear a second hand covering—finger gloves of wool or soft leather. The mittens must have gauntlets and should be attached to a string that you either place around your neck or thread through one coat sleeve and out the other—the same arrangement mothers use for toddlers who constantly misplace things. Working around camp, you'll be continually removing the mittens both to function better and to cool off. Without the safety harness, you'll be sure to misplace at least one within minutes.

■ Foot protection begins with cotton or silk socks next to the skin, followed by one or two pairs of rag-knit wool socks. Fresh socks are used for sleeping at night while those used during the day dry out. An alternate foot covering for use inside the sleeping bag and tent is the down bootie.

■ The warmest commercially made lightweight boot for winter camping consists of a rubber shoepac with nylon or vinyl uppers. Inside are full duffel or felt booties that can be removed. For rain or snow, the same inner boots can be used inside all-rubber outers.

■ If you are caught unprepared in weather that is turning quickly colder, stuff grass, weeds, rushes—anything available—into your jacket. These natural materials make excellent insulation—and just might save your life.

■ A down sleeping bag's full potential is realized when the bag is used on a foam mattress instead of an air mattress which permits a wide chilled space to remain under your kidneys. When using a bag on a cot, try putting heavy-duty aluminum foil or one of the modern pocket survival-type blankets beneath the bag for extra warmth. There is also a cot which comes with down insulation on its underside.

■ Down sleeping bags should be sponged off with mild soap and tepid water when they become spot-soiled. For a major cleaning (not often needed), you can wash the bag in the above solution and hang it in a mesh bag or hammock outdoors, fluffing it up frequently with your hands as it dries. You can also dry it in an automatic drier set on low. Or the sleeping robe may be dry-cleaned. Just make sure the dry cleaner uses a petroleum-based cleaner, not chlorinated hydrocarbons that remove the natural oil from the down. And if you intend to have the bag waterproofed, make sure the outfit you choose to do the job uses the spray method instead of the total-immersion method.

■ Never wear yellow or amber lenses on sun-bright days in snow. They are designed for dull days to bring out detail, and wearing them in the sun is a severe strain. Equip yourself with snow goggles having dark lenses and side protection if you will be out for several days. And it's a good idea to carry a spare pair of regular sunglasses in case something happens to the goggles.

■ Hiking on even gentle-sloped mountains where packed snow and ice exist is made much easier with the aid of a small ice axe. This tool may also save you from a nasty fall on slippery terrain. Such axes are reasonably priced and available in mountaineering-supply stores and from many mail-order houses.

■ You can use almost any tent for winter camping as long as it is made of modern, "breathable" material. Fatal accidents have occurred when the old waterproofed-canvas tents were snowed over, causing their occupants to be asphyxiated. The best tents for camping in truly high altitudes or severe winter conditions are those that have either a waterproof fly fully covering them or a built-in double roof. The waterproof top layer of such tents may ice over completely without endangering the occupants since there is an air space between layers and the breathable underroof is completely free of rime.

■ When cooking or using a heater inside a tent, always assure yourself of good ventilation. Even the smallest stoves can rapidly use up available oxygen. A greater danger is from carbon-monoxide poisoning. A cookstove burning in a confined space that lacks a good oxygen supply will give off carbon monoxide. This colorless, odorless gas gives no hint of its presence save sometimes a faint pressure in the temples. This, of course, is not to warn against cooking inside your tent. You have to in really cold weather. Just make sure that when heavy snow is falling, your ventilation opening does not become clogged. Check often.

■ Exterior zippers that worked perfectly during mild weather often have the annoying habit of jamming or freezing in the cold. Most experienced winter campers prefer a tent that has at least one snow-tunnel entrance. This is nothing more than a sleevelike arrangement in one end of the tent; it's sealed or opened by means of a simple drawstring.

■ A tent that has a small opening in its floor will be an aid if you are using a one-burner backpack-type stove. Placing the stove over the opening will not only keep heat from the fabric but it will also save a great deal of soiling from inevitable spilled food. In some tents, these holes can be snapped closed when not in use, in others a nylon zipper is provided for that purpose.

■ If a great deal of cooking is to be done inside the tent, choose a shelter that has two entrances so that people will not constantly be climbing over the cook.

■ When tents have been set up on snow for several days, snowmelt will frequently begin to ooze in where the sleeping bags touch the tent walls. This problem can be eliminated by sewing a nine-inch strip of coated waterproof fabric along the inside lower wall.

■ If you're traveling in snow deep enough to require snowshoes or skis, make sure you pack down the area on which the tent is to be erected. An area larger than the size of the tent is needed since you'll be going in and out without the footwear that kept you on top.

■ Even if you have first packed down the snow to be under the tent, the tent will still slowly begin to settle after any length of time. To avoid having the slimmer (thus faster-sinking) poles go down ahead of the tent, attach them to the corners of the shelter. You can do this by fixing a grommet into the tent-pole loop and a short prong into the pole bottom. The prong fits into the grommet. If the tent does not have a loop, just attach a cord from the corner to the pole.

■ Making water from snow is not always as easy as one might think. To do it, make a pile of clean snow. Scoop snow from this pile into a pot on your stove or fire. When water begins to ooze through the surface of the snow in the pot, put more in, pushing the melting portion down to the bottom. If you wait until the top layer has completely melted before you add more, you may find that much of the bottom water has evaporated and that the pot is scorched. Allow more time than you think you'll need; this chore is a slow one.

31

Snowmobiling

Snowmobiles have widened winter horizons immensely. In addition to furnishing great winter sport, the machines have become vital links with the outside world in areas visited by severe snowstorms. Law enforcement personnel and conservation officials use them in their work. And they serve all in cases of emergency when snows have cut off normal means of transportation.

However, there are those who have done little to keep snowmobiling's name in a favorable light. It falls on the shoulders of serious users of the machines to counteract any bad press given to the sport. This can be done not only by adhering rigidly to codes set up by responsible snowmobilers and their organizations but by going out of the way to offer assistance and small courtesies to those who open their lands to snowmobile use. It cannot be overemphasized that snowmobilers must show concern for the land over which they ride and for the wildlife that lives there. If this is done, the snowmobile will continue to have a place in winter sports for years to come.

■ In very cold weather, starting fluid (ether) will take the strain out of coaxing reluctant engines to life. Carry a small can of it in your emergency kit. After a five-second dose in the carburetor, followed by a quick choke, your machine should start easily.

■ If you've forgotten starting fluid, try this method to ensure easy starts in frigid weather. Instead of simply turning off the ignition to shut down the machine at night, full-choke it. This procedure will stop the engine by causing excess vapor to form in the carburetor. The vapor will ignite quickly the next day to start your snowmobile fast.

■ A spark plug that fouls somewhere out in the backcountry will end your fun faster than a spring shower's melting the last good snow of the season. If you forgot spare plugs, you can easily clean the gummed one with a rag or, better, an emery board or nail file. It's smart to keep one taped to your machine. Follow this cleaning with a squirt of gasoline into the piston chamber, replace the plug and with one good pull on the starter cord, you should be on your way.

■ The most frequent cause of snowmobile accidents appears to be collisions with automobiles. It should not even be necessary to say that the snow machines have no place on highways, but there are always a few winter warriors who seem compelled to race along the main vehicular arteries or on medians of divided highways. No snowmobiler should operate his rig on public roadways, shoulders or inside banks or slopes of county, state or U.S. highways unless extremely heavy snows have rendered such a road completely impassable for automobiles and trucks. When it's necessary to cross a main route, first turn on your lights and then, with the snowmobile at a ninety-degree angle to the road, make a complete stop and yield to all traffic.

■ Many who operate their machines in the company of others have wished for some sort of rearview mirror. To date, the experimental ones have proved fairly impractical. However, one maker may have come up with a solution in the form of a no-shatter plastic mirror that attaches to the driver's arm instead of the snowmobile steering handle.

■ Before each start, check your spring-loaded throttle to make sure it moves freely and returns to the fully closed position automatically. Starting a machine with a frozen or otherwise stuck throttle can send your snowmobile hurtling out of control.

■ Learn the distances required to bring your snowmobile to a stop at various speeds under various snow and ice conditions. Remember, unlike a car that generally operates on hard pavement, snowmobiles always run on a slick surface that has an infinitely greater degree of variability than blacktop.

■ If you do much night driving, apply reflective tape not only to your machine but also to your clothing and helmet. Besides making you easier to spot while you are driving, it also increases the ease with which other drivers can see you if you should step away from your machine in the dark.

■ If trouble develops in your braking system, throttle control or carburetion system, preventing you from slowing down or stopping, just turn your ignition key or emergency switch to the "off" position. You'll then be able to steer your machine as it coasts to a safe stop.

■ This tip seems so basic it ought not to be necessary to mention it: There are *no* conditions under which the practice of checking fuel-tank levels with a match or cigarette lighter is safe—even when the tank is empty and there is no breeze. Remember, it's the vapors that explode, not the liquid gasoline. Always carry a small flashlight for this job, and make a practice of looking for and eliminating fuel leaks. Wipe up spilled fuel immediately.

■ In severe weather, warm the oil you'll be mixing with the gasoline for your vehicle. This enables the two liquids to combine more thoroughly. Always keep away from idling machines while you're making the mixture. Never add fuel to a running snowmobile.

■ Beginning drivers sometimes make the mistake of estimating cruising range of their vehicle on a strict miles-per-gallon or hours-per-gallon basis. The veterans know that snow and terrain conditions can vary sharply from day to day. They've learned how much fuel their machines consume in different situations and are therefore better able to judge cruising ranges for a given area with particular snow conditions. And they always carry reserve fuel.

■ Minimum safety equipment that should be carried on snowmobile trips consists of:
> **Emergency rations (energy snacks, freeze-dried foods)**
> **First-aid kit**
> **Flares**
> **Flashlight**
> **Knife or small ax**
> **Pair of snowshoes (the plastic type is O.K.)**
> **Spare drive belt**
> **Spare fuel**
> **Spare socks**
> **Spark plugs**
> **Tool kit**
> **Waterproof matches**

■ Assume a kneeling position (using one or both knees to bear your weight) for riding over rough terrain. This will soften the jolts your spine must absorb, putting much of the burden on your leg muscles. When you've had sufficient experience to handle the machine with perfect control, a standing position is acceptable for traveling over extremely rough ground or while negotiating uphill grades.

■ Stuck in deep snow on an uphill run? Here's the approved method for getting out of such a situation. Turn off the engine. Free the skis from the downhill side. Slide the rear of the machine onto undisturbed snow, then motor out with slow, even throttle pressure. Determined to keep going? Try scooping the skis out from the front end. Then stand upright on the snowmobile running board, keeping your weight as far back as possible, and rock the machine from side

35

to side as you slowly accelerate. This method packs the snow, giving maximum track contact and traction.

■ When pulling a sleigh loaded with equipment or persons, use a rigid-hitch tow bar instead of rope—a rope can become entangled in the track or drive mechanism of the tow vehicle. Variable snow and ice conditions or inexperience in proper driving technique can give rope-towed sleds an unpleasant crack-the-whip propulsion or send them caroming into the rear of the snowmobile.

■ Remember the wind-chill factor when dressing for snowmobile jaunts. If the wind is at calm, for example, and it is thirty degrees Fahrenheit, a speed of twenty-five miles per hour can knock the temperature to the equivalent of zero. Always bring ski-type face masks on snowmobile trips (the "chamois" or suede leather ones provide the most protection), and avoid long scarves that can catch in moving parts of the machine. Besides your helmet, bring an additional head covering, such as a stocking cap or balaclava, that can be pulled over your ears. Eye protection in the form of goggles is a must and safety goggles are very worthwhile. The best footwear is rubber-bottomed, nylon- or leather-topped boots with felt liners. One-piece coverall-type snowmobile suits offer the best wind check for the torso.

WIND-CHILL FACTOR

ESTIMATED WIND SPEED IN MPH	ACTUAL THERMOMETER READING (°F.)										
	50	40	30	20	10	0	-10	-20	-30	-40	-50	-60
	EQUIVALENT TEMPERATURE (°F.)										
calm	50	40	30	20	10	0	-10	-20	-30	-40	-50	-60
5	48	37	27	16	6	-5	-15	-26	-36	-47	-57	-68
10	40	28	16	4	-9	-21	-33	-46	-58	-70	-83	-95
15	36	22	9	-5	-18	-36	-45	-58	-72	-85	-99	-112
20	32	18	4	-10	-25	-39	-53	-67	-82	-96	-110	-124
25	30	16	0	-15	-29	-44	-59	-74	-88	-104	-118	-133
30	28	13	-2	-18	-33	-48	-63	-79	-94	-109	-125	-140
35	27	11	-4	-20	-35	-49	-67	-82	-98	-113	-129	-145
40	26	10	-6	-21	-37	-53	-69	-85	-100	-116	-132	-148

(wind speeds greater than 40 mph have little additional effect.)

LITTLE DANGER (for properly clothed person)   INCREASING DANGER   GREAT DANGER

(danger from freezing of exposed flesh)

■ The second most common cause of snowmobile mishaps is ice breakthrough. When snowmobiles are used in conjunction with ice fishing and other frozen-water activities, extreme caution is mandatory. Even if an area of ice is supporting fishermen's shanties, people and all sorts of heavy gear, nearby ice may still be risky; remember, no one has ever guaranteed that ice of *any* thickness will support a snowmobile.

■ If your tilt-bed snowmobile-carrying trailer does not come with a hand winch, have an inexpensive one installed. Don't drive your machine onto such a trailer; many serious accidents have resulted when misjudgment or a little extra throttle squeeze caused the snowmobile to power up and over the trailer to smash into the back of the towing car.

■ You can convert a boat trailer to a snowmobile trailer by removing the rollers and cradle pads and then bolting on a four- by eight-foot sheet of three-quarter-inch outdoor plywood. Eye bolts are used as anchors fore and aft, strong Dacron or nylon line for tiedown.

■ A good windbreak for use when ice fishing, picnicking or camping with snowmobiles can be easily built. Materials include three poles of three-and-a-half feet each (conduit works well) and a piece of canvas or nylon, three feet four inches wide and as long as the seat on your snowmobile.

Lay the poles parallel to each other on the ground and space them evenly. Attach the material flat along the poles, flush to the top. This will leave two inches of exposed poles at the bottom. Three small pieces of pipe, slightly larger in diameter than the poles, are then bolted vertically to the frame of the snowmobile along one side. The poles fit into these or any other makeshift brackets, forming a windscreen, allowing you to utilize the snowmobile seat fully

37

protected from prevailing winds. When out of use, the screen is furled, lashed and stowed alongside, out of the way.

■ Frequently traveled snowmobile trails inevitably develop roller-coaster bumps and dips. Here's how to make your own grader to give favorite routes near-superhighway smoothness, no matter what their previous condition. Materials:

    2 two-by-fours, each 12 feet long
    20 carriage bolts, each ⅝₁₆ inch by 2 ½ inches
    5 angle-iron sections, each 30 inches long
    (The type of angle iron used in bed frames is perfect.)
    3 feet of towing chain

The two-by-fours are laid flat and parallel. Angle-iron pieces are spaced evenly, then bolted between the lumber (two bolts to an end) so that one edge of each iron juts at right angles to the wood. This

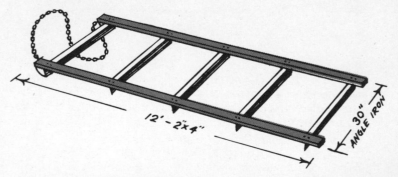

edge is the scraping blade. Ends of the chain are attached to each two-by-four for towing. Two pieces of metal may be bent in the form of ski tips or sleigh runners and fastened to the front edge of each two-by-four to enable this sledlike grader to run more easily over snow.

Outdoor
Cooking

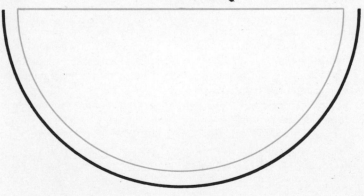

Although there are those who feel that having an overabundance of home comforts takes much of the fun out of camping, most people feel that the more work that can be cut from camping chores, especially cooking, the more time there is for fun. Insulated luncheon coolers; heavy-duty aluminum foil; light, compact, reliable camp stoves that have genuinely controllable heat as well as a sufficient number of burners and an easy fueling process; nonstick-coated pots and pans; dehydrated soup mixes that, when prepared, taste homemade and freeze-dried foods that taste like fresh foods are only a partial list of recent developments designed to make outdoor living easier.

■ Freshly caught fish can appear on your menu even when the outing isn't ostensibly a fishing trip. On a hike, drive or camping trip, pack a little take-down fly rod or spinning rod in case you spot a likely looking stream or pond. Panfish provide good sport on very light tackle, and they're delicious. If the catch is too small for conventional filleting or frying, try an easy-way sauté. Just clean the cavity, leaving the head, fins and tail attached. Wipe each fish dry, roll it in flour and season it with salt and pepper. Then melt a little (not too much) bacon fat or butter in a skillet over a medium-hot fire, and your fish will brown beautifully in about ten minutes.

■ In this day of fancy poultry—when you can't find much dark meat on a chicken—game birds are an outdoor gourmet's delight. Sometimes in the fall you can even decide what to hunt on the basis of what you'd like to eat. Prefer white meat? You won't go wrong with a pheasant, especially a young one. Prefer dark meat? You'll find it on birds that do a lot of flying—doves and ducks, for example—because their blood has a high content of oxygen-storing myoglobin, which is what makes the meat dark.

■ Certain staples, seasonings and foods that keep relatively well and can be used in a variety of dishes are highly recommended for outdoor cooking, particularly on camping trips. These include dry soup mixes, bouillon cubes or powder, canned fruits and vegetables (*small* cans, both for variety and for easy packing in odd corners and pockets), canned bacon, shortening, fresh onions, carrots, potatoes, rice, noodles and/or spaghetti, baking powder, baking soda, flour, salt, pepper, poultry seasoning and garlic salt. One carefully marked packet or container of the flour can be preseasoned with salt and pepper. If you and your family like to add both salt and pepper to most dishes, you can mix the two together in one shaker and tape the top to prevent its spilling. Use about three parts salt to one part pepper. Other items that taste good, keep well and are relatively light and compact include just about all the freeze-dried and instant foods; powdered soft-drink concentrates; prepared mixes for pancakes, biscuits, muffins and corn bread; dehydrated milk and eggs for cooking and baking (use fresh for drinking and eating), plus snacks, such as dried fruits, nuts, caramel corn and crackers. Butter keeps better than most people realize. Chunk bacon keeps better than the sliced kind. Cocoa makes powdered milk palatable and can also be used in making puddings. Concentrated foods and soups make fine sauces when used with about half the water normally added. A light sprinkling of paprika (the mild kind if you're not a paprika fan) aids in browning fish.

■ Figure out how much food per day each person in your family normally consumes, and on this basis make up menus and lists of staples in advance of your camping trip. You'll have no problem at all if you'll be traveling in a rec vehicle and can stop in towns along the way to replenish your larder or if your camper has a fair-sized icebox or refrigerator. But if you're going to be in the wilds for a while, you'll have to figure on using perishables first and plan meals accordingly. A first-day breakfast might be fruit juice, bacon and eggs, toast and milk or coffee. Lunch might consist of sliced tomatoes and cucumbers, cold cuts, potato chips or sticks, cookies, milk, coffee or tea. Dinner could include chicken, fresh green beans and potatoes, fresh cake, coffee. By the third day, breakfast might be fresh citrus fruit (which keeps fairly well), ham, pancakes or French toast and coffee. Lunch might be cheese, canned luncheon meat or canned tuna, coffee or tea. Dinner might be stew, roasted corn, biscuits, canned fruit or pudding, coffee or tea. When the fresh fruit begins to go soft or become discolored, it will have to be used up. At that point you'll want to have canned fruit along.

■ If you're worried about packing easily broken eggs, break them beforehand and put them—without the shells—in a wide-mouthed plastic jar with a screw-on cap. You may not be able to keep all the yolks intact, but those that disintegrate can be used for making scrambled eggs, French toast or as a cooking ingredient in other dishes.

■ Stale bread and powdered eggs will make fine French toast.

■ You may plan to use a portable camp stove most of the time, but there will be times when cooking over a wood fire will be more fun. Doing so can also improve the taste of some foods—corn or potatoes, for example, or meat grilled or barbecued over the right woods. The best wood varieties are the hardwoods, such as oak, hickory, ash, maple and fruit woods. These are known as sweet woods in reference to the good flavor they impart. The resin in some of the soft woods will impart an astringent or even turpentine-like taste—avoid them for cooking purposes or wait until they've burned down to charcoal embers.

■ Ingenious campers have come up with a variety of fire-starters. Here are a few of the best. Before leaving home, fill a half-pint milk carton with sand or sawdust, saturate the contents with kerosene, tape the container's mouth closed and seal the whole works in a plastic bag to prevent evaporation. Pack the bag with your charcoal. To make a quick cooking fire, put the bag in the fireplace and touch a match to it; then just pour the charcoal over it. Another fine fire-starter can be fashioned by breaking dry corn cobs (save your roasting ears) in half and dipping them in melted paraffin. You'll need only one or two pieces per fire, and they can be stored cleanly in any bag. It's best to heat paraffin outdoors, by the way, in a pan several inches deep—and keep the stuff away from an open flame while heating it. Another method is to cut newspaper into strips about four inches wide, roll them tightly into small-diameter "logs," and saturate each one in paraffin or ordinary leftover candle wax. Then put them in a cool, dry place until the coating hardens. The logs will light easily and burn for quite a while, providing fuel as well as a starter. In an emergency, the tube of rubber cement you pack along for temporary repairs will also start a fire. Be careful with it—it's quite flammable. Just squeeze some onto small bits of wood (you won't need much, if any, real tinder) and light them. The flame will be hot enough to start the larger wood. It will smell a little at first, but the odor will be dissipated by the time you're ready to cook. Any of these starters will eliminate the need to carry a big can of commercial charcoal-starting liquid.

■ When charcoal is spread out, it takes a long time for all the pieces to get sufficiently hot and begin glowing uniformly. The process is quickened when a container is used that will provide a draft like a chimney. Make such a container by cutting both ends out of a two- or three-pound coffee can. Then punch four holes, each about the size of a quarter, around one end, about one-and-a-half inches from the rim or base. Set the can (holes down) in the center of your fireplace or charcoal broiler. Stuff in some loose paper, dump as much charcoal as you think you'll need on top of the paper and add fire-starter. Light it and you'll have red-hot coals very soon. Being careful not to burn your fingers—use mitts if you have them—lift the can off the coals, spread the coals and start cooking.

■ Keep a water-filled clothes sprinkler at your fireplace or grill. In case fat drippings make the flames shoot up, a fast sprinkling will quickly and safely tame the flames, and the spray can be directed precisely enough to avoid wetting down your food.

■ To estimate fire temperature for grilling, hold your hand, palm down, a couple of inches above the grid. If you have to withdraw your hand in less than three seconds, the fire is hot—about four hundred degrees. If you can hold your hand there for almost another second, the temperature is about three hundred fifty degrees. It's about three hundred degrees if you can hold your hand over it for four to five seconds. For most purposes, you want a steady, medium-low to medium temperature, but for deep frying, you need very hot oil. Deep-fried fish fillets are particularly delicious when cooked only after you have enough heat to produce sizzling hot oil. To test the temperature of the oil, drop in a small piece of bread. If it starts to brown in about a minute, put in the fish. If not, wait a bit. Another way to test it is to put in a very small chunk of the fish itself. It should bubble and sizzle and quickly start browning.

■ If you're going to cook over a wood or charcoal fire rather than on a portable stove, pack along a reflector oven. Light, compactly foldable reflector ovens are available at camping-goods stores. Set up such an oven on ground about a foot or a foot and a half from the fire so that the sloping top and bottom as well as the sides of the device will reflect heat onto the horizontal shelf located across its center. The food to be cooked is placed on this shelf. The uniform heat will cook just about anything evenly and well, but it is particularly good for baking muffins, biscuits, pies, cakes, bread and even spuds. The oven should be placed with its back to the wind to shield the fire, and you'll get the best baking results not by timing the food but by watching it. If foods get too hot too fast, just move the oven back. To boost the heat and retard rusting, you can line the reflecting walls with aluminum foil.

■ Before you roast a potato in the coals, wrap it in foil or put it inside an empty can that has the lid still slightly attached. The potato will come out well roasted and clean. Corn can also be wrapped in foil for roasting. It will be tastier if you leave a few of the husks wrapped around it.

■ With or without a foil covering to boost the temperature, you can fashion a cooking reflector from a short plank or flat-surfaced piece of wood. Using rocks, prop the plank at about a forty-five-degree angle to the fire and a foot or so away. Then nail or prop fish fillets or slabs of meat flat on the plank to cook.

■ Rocks used in or near a fire should be dry. Those taken from a stream bank or damp ground may hold enough moisture to make them crack or even explode when they get really hot.

■ If your camper is not stove-equipped but does have enough space for one more piece of equipment, a portable camp stove could be considered an essential. Its size and the number of burners it has will depend on your family's needs; some camping families find it most convenient to carry two such stoves—a one-burner and a two-burner—rather than a single, larger three-burner model. There are also much bigger indoor camp stoves available for use in a large tent at a campsite that will be occupied for extended periods, but the small folding types are best for most camping.

■ There are three fuel systems available for portable camp stoves: alcohol, gasoline (white, leaded or naptha) and propane (LP). Although the little alcohol-burner is extremely safe and great for backpacking, it is too small for general camp use. Some camp chefs like a gasoline stove because the heat can be precisely regulated (in the same way you regulate your home range), but gasoline requires pumping to build up air pressure in the tank. The most popular type is propane, employing inexpensively refillable tanks or replaceable cylinders. Such a stove requires no pumping —just turn on or off—and many models can be easily adjusted to obtain the desired heat.

■ Another indispensable item whenever you have room for it is an insulated cooler, or ice chest. It's astounding how long a cooler will keep ice solid, salad crisp, bread fresh and drinks cool. Small and very light models, made of unreinforced plastic, are all right for picnics—or even camping trips if durability isn't a consideration— but they won't stand up very well. The somewhat more expensive and slightly heavier type, with urethane-foam insulation protected by an enameled steel or aluminum exterior and a plastic inner wall, should withstand years of rigorous use.

■ Still another valuable kind of camp-cooking gear is a nesting set of aluminum utensils (pots, saucepans, pie pans, skillets, etc.) matched by a nesting service of cups and plates and a nesting set of plastic storage containers with tight-sealing lids. When nested together with the smaller items inside the larger ones, all these things pack up into one or two light, easily transported units.

■ A pot can serve nicely as a dishpan. After it's used, wash it well and then sanitize it by drying it in front of the fire.

■ Immediately after taking cooked food from a pot or pan, fill the utensil with water, add a little soap and put it back on the fire.

The remaining bits of food in it won't harden and stick, and by the time you've finished eating, you'll have hot, soapy dishwater.

■ Although food won't stick to nonstick-coated utensils, those without a coating can be a problem to clean if you're without steel wool or some other abrasive. An excellent substitute scraper is a medium-sized pine cone. Incidentally, nonstick-coated pans have other uses besides frying. Their size, shape and surface make them excellent salad or dessert molds.

■ If your family won't abide by Mrs. Izaak Walton's golden rule, "He who catches 'em, scales 'em and cleans 'em," you need help. Here are some scaling tips. If you don't have a scaler or fish knife in camp, hold a common table fork upright on the fish, with the tines toward you, and scrape away, working from the tail to the head. Then pour water over the fish to flush off any loosened scales that remain. The crimped type of bottle caps that must be removed with a bottle opener make an even better substitute scaler. Just screw three of them in a row to a chunk of wood for a handle. The flat tops go against the wood, of course, so that the rough, crimped edges can be rubbed along the fish for scaling.

■ To hold a fish in place for scaling or filleting, pin it (near the tail) to a log or board with a narrow-pointed knife, an awl or an ice pick.

■ Fish that require little or no skinning or scaling (trout, char and salmon, for instance) can be cleaned very quickly with a sharp knife. Starting at the vent, make a slit straight up the underside to the base of the tongue. Cut around and then grasp the tongue with one hand while holding the head with the other. Now just pull apart, removing the viscera all at once. It will take only another moment to scrape away the black kidney material along the top of the body cavity. The fish will keep better if you wipe the cavity dry with a paper towel. (Paper towels have many uses, from drying fish to wiping hands to starting fires—fold a few and stow them in your pocket.)

■ After a large fish has been cleaned and scaled, steaks for broiling, baking or frying can be cut quickly and easily. Simply slice down from the top of the back through the belly, beginning at the head and working back, slice by slice, in whatever thicknesses you desire.

■ Filleting takes a bit more finesse, but this method eliminates the need to eviscerate your catch. Use a knife that isn't too sharp because you want to work it under the skin without cutting through. Lay the fish on its side, on a cutting board or log. Make the first cut behind the head, down to the backbone. Then turn the blade toward the tail, and with a sawing motion, cut along the backbone and rib cage almost to the tail. Turn the cut slab back, over the tail, and saw your way back to the first cut, sliding the knife between flesh and skin. That is the first fillet. For the second, turn the fish over and repeat. The head, skin, viscera, bones and tail remain linked, ready to dispose of.

■ A knife soon loses its edge when it is used to cut through the bones of game. Poultry shears or tin snips are excellent for quartering birds and also for dressing small furred game.

■ After plucking and dressing a game bird, hold it up to a bright light to detect any buried shot pellets. Pick them out when possible because it's no fun to bite down on lead. A good tool for picking out shot can be fashioned from a large building nail. Flatten its point to a butter-knife shape by placing it in a vise or by hammering it on rock or a cement floor. Don't break off the tip in the process; it should remain sharp.

■ When preparing game birds, wet-plucking is generally easier and faster than dry-plucking. The most primitive wet-plucking technique is merely to dip the bird in almost-scalding water and then to pluck away. This will do nicely on easily plucked birds. For slightly tougher jobs, add a little liquid soap or about half a cup of soap flakes to three gallons of water before heating it. The soap will penetrate the oil of the feathers and allow the water to soak right in up to the skin. Submerge the bird for half a minute or so, then rinse it in cold water and proceed to pluck. Even better—especially for big, hard-to-pluck birds like geese—is flaked paraffin. Buy it already flaked or shave ordinary paraffin. To use this method, bring a large bucket of water to a boil, sprinkle the flakes in and, when they've melted but the water is still very hot, dip your bird in the solution. Pull the bird out and let it cool for a minute or rinse it in cold water. You'll find that a paraffin coating has hardened on and among the feathers, sticking them together in large masses that pull away from the skin quite easily. It will now take only a couple of minutes to completely defeather the bird. Warning: Do not pour the leftover paraffin solution down any drain. It will quickly cool and solidify, causing a monumental stoppage. Let it cool and harden in the bucket, then skim it off and discard it with the feathers before pouring out the water.

■ Either wet- or dry-plucking will be easier if you wear a rubber thimble of the kind used by bankers for counting paper money.

■ To prevent plucked feathers from drifting about and settling on everything in sight, use a large plastic garbage or dry-cleaning bag. (If you use the latter, tape the small hanger opening closed.) Sit down with the bag placed between your legs, and tape each side to your legs to keep it open. Then hold the bird inside the bag while you pluck away.

■ Both small and large furred game should be field-dressed as soon after shooting as possible to release the body heat. Chill the meat and keep it cool until it's either frozen or cooked.

■ Soaking game meat in water or brine will do little to tenderize it; in fact, this kind of soaking may make it stringy. Soaking it in an appropriate marinade, on the other hand, will tenderize it and bring out the flavor.

■ Hang a shoe bag from a low tree limb or tack it to a wash stand or table in your outdoor camp kitchen. The shoe pockets are great for holding easily mislaid items, such as spatulas, ladles, containers for seasoning, etc.

■ It's easy to make a frame with hangers to hold kettles and pots at a desired height above a grill or fire. Drive two long, forked sticks into the ground on each side of the fireplace. The forked ends should be at least three feet above the ground. Lay a sapling pole across the forks. Now find a few small limbs which branch at a sufficiently acute angle to form a hook. Hook these over the crosspole and notch their other ends to hold pot handles. If you make a series of notches, you will be able to adjust the elevations of the pots. Either use green wood or make the rack high enough and wide enough that it won't eventually start smoldering.

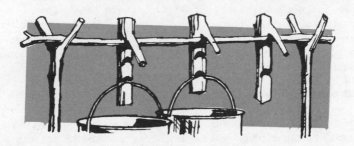

■ When cooked, a frozen fish can taste almost as good as a freshly caught one—*if* it's frozen properly. As soon as possible after the fish is caught, clean it and immediately seal it in a plastic bag. Freeze it. Then promptly put it, bag and all, in a plastic milk carton. Fill the carton with cold water and put it back in the freezer. Your fish will keep indefinitely, and there should be no freezer burn.

■ Venison and other game meats can be canned in the following manner: Cut the meat into cubes (about an inch or so square). Season each cube with salt and pepper as you pack it—uncooked —into a sterilized canning jar. When the jar is about a quarter full, add a medium-sized cube or chunk of bacon or salt pork. Then add more venison and another chunk of bacon, maintaining the same proportions, until the jar is filled to within a half-inch of the top. Seal it tightly. Although the cooking can be done in a water-filled

49

pressure cooker (follow manufacturer's directions) or in an ordinary water-filled pot on top of the range, some cooks prefer to use an oven. If you use the last method, place the jar in a water-filled pot and allow it to cook, at about three hundred sixty degrees, for three to three-and-a-half hours. After removing it from the oven, don't tamper with the seal of a jar unless you plan to eat some of the meat and then put the jar in the refrigerator. It must remain sealed to keep. Meat canned in this simple way is great when served creamed, in a casserole or in buns with barbecue sauce.

■ Although we do not recommend hunting for mushrooms unless you're an expert *and* have a detailed field guide to the edible and inedible varieties, there are many other wild foods that are safe to pick for eating. Among the more obvious ones are nuts, blueberries, wild raspberries, watercress, rose hips, purslane and wild grapes. Wild onions are delicious (and loaded with vitamin C); they have a slightly different taste from that of domestic varieties. They are fine when served raw in salads or when served cooked in poached dishes and chowders. Other plants whose leaves and shoots are tasty and nourishing include chicory, milkweed, clover, dandelion, great burdock and fiddlehead ferns. When boiled, the last-named plant is as tasty as asparagus.

■ Sourdough flapjacks, bread and biscuits are good camp fare. To make your sourdough starter, mix a packet of dry yeast with a cup of flour and a cup of warm water in a crock or glass jar (never in a metal container). Let it stand for a day, covered lightly with a cloth, in a warm spot. That night add two more cups of flour and two more cups of warm water, again mixing thoroughly. Let it stand overnight and it will be ready. Be sure to return one cup of mixture to your starter jar each time you make a sourdough food and you will be ready to prepare your next recipe. Here are some tasty sourdough specialties for you to try.

SOURDOUGH BREAD

To your starter, add enough flour and lukewarm water—equal amounts of each—to give you a total of about 3 cups of mixture. Let this stand in a warm place overnight—or, at least, for 6 to 8 hours. Take out 2 cups of this sponge to use for your baking and put the rest aside—that's your starter for next time.

4 cups flour	1 teaspoon salt
2 tablespoons sugar	2 tablespoons shortening, melted

Mix together the flour, sugar and salt. Make a well in the center of the mixture and pour in the melted shortening. Put the 2 cups of sponge into the well and mix with shortening; then blend well with the flour mixture. You should have a soft dough. If not, add flour or liquid—water or milk. Knead for 3 or 4 minutes on any clean, floured surface. Cut off chunks of the dough to fit the pans you are going to use, and put in a warm place to rise. When doubled in bulk, bake 50 to 60 minutes in a moderately hot oven or reflector baker—preferably one that is hottest in the first 15 minutes. Test with a straw—if it comes out dry, the bread is done.

SOURDOUGH FLAPJACKS

Add 2 cups of flour and 2 cups of lukewarm water to sourdough starter and leave to rise overnight in a warm, draft-free place. In the morning take out the original amount of starter and save it.

2 eggs (fresh or dried)	1 teaspoon warm water
½ teaspoon salt	2 tablespoons shortening
1 tablespoon sugar	(melted or liquid)
1 teaspoon baking soda	

Mix eggs, salt and sugar with a fork. Dissolve soda in water. Stir egg mixture, dissolved soda and shortening into sourdough batter. If the batter is too thick to pour, thin it with a little milk. Grease a hot griddle or frying pan lightly with bacon rind. Pour out flapjacks; turn when starting to show small bubbles. Turn only once; the second side should take only half as long as the first to cook.

SOURDOUGH MUFFINS

Set the sponge the night before; in the morning take out the starter.

1½ cups whole wheat flour	1 cup raisins (optional)
½ cup sugar	½ cup shortening
1 teaspoon salt	(melted or liquid)
¼ cup dry milk powder	2 eggs
1½ teaspoons baking soda	

Mix together flour, sugar, salt, milk powder and soda. Add raisins—or wild blueberries or other berries if you have them. Make a well in the center of these dry ingredients and mix the egg and shortening in it. Stir into dry ingredients, with sponge, to blend. Pour into greased muffin tins and bake in hot oven or reflector baker 20 minutes or until they are done when tested with a straw.

■ Although older game birds may require parboiling to tenderize them, small or young ones are excellent broiled or roasted. Because wild birds are lean, baste them much more generously than you would domestic poultry. If you don't, the meat will be dry. Butter, suet or bacon fat is good for basting. Steaming will also keep them moist.

■ When roasting a bird, put it on the oven's center grill. Below it, place a large saucepan filled with vegetables, such as carrots, onions, celery, potatoes, turnips or parsnips if you like them, the usual seasoning and—for an unusual treat—assorted nuts. Fill the pan with just enough water to cover the vegetables. Its rising steam will help keep the bird moist, and a strip or two of bacon pinned to the breast will complete the job. When the roasting is done, the vegetables can be served just as they come from the oven. But a better idea is to put a generous portion of them, along with the remaining water, in the container of a blender. It will whip into one of the best gravies you have ever had.

■ Kabobs are naturals for camp dinners. On metal skewers or sharpened hardwood stakes, they can be grilled over a stove or fire without using a single pot or pan. A good order for the items on the skewer is as follows: a chunk of meat; a small piece of strip bacon; a small, partially boiled (still firm) potato; a small whole onion or a thick slice of onion; another chunk of meat; another piece of bacon and more vegetables. Additional items that may be interspersed with these on the skewer are whole mushrooms and large slices of green pepper. Saffron rice (cooked separately, of course) makes a good bed on which to serve the kabob.

■ Because water boils at relatively low temperatures in high altitudes, food will take longer to cook. Be patient or speed it up a little by clamping a pot lid on tight with a few alligator clips (the clips used by electricians).

■ A wire corn popper is a fine utensil in camp. In addition to popping corn, it can be used to roast hot dogs over a fire. Not as much of the tasty juice will be lost as when they are roasted on a stick or fork.

■ Foil has many other cooking uses. Bend a wire coat hanger (mentioned earlier as being a fine camp convenience) into a circle with a handle. Cover the circle with heavy foil, crimped over the edges, to make a serviceable skillet. Heavy foil can also be shaped into a saucepan or shallow pot or used to wrap foods to be roasted in the coals.

■ For a different and wonderful taste, slice a roasted potato, either peeled or unpeeled, and put it back together with slices of cheese between the potato slices. Then wrap it in foil and reheat.

■ The old Midwestern prejudice against eating northern pike— "snake fish," as the species is called by those who disdain it—is a shame. Pike is as good as it is bony, and the bone problem is easily solved. Cut the fish into slabs as you would in conventional filleting, but leave the skin on. Then about every half-inch make cuts through the flesh down to the skin but not through it. In a skillet, heat bacon fat or cooking oil for deep frying. When the oil is hot enough, hold the slab of fish by the ends, bend them back a little and pull them open (as if you were working an accordion), thus opening up the pleats you've cut. Slowly submerge the fish in the hot oil and fry it. The small remaining bones in the flesh will fry like potato chips. They'll taste good, and they can be harmlessly crunched and eaten with the rest of the fish.

■ Certain meats—fish in particular—have a tendency to stick to a skillet. Sprinkle salt on the skillet before putting the fish on or add a dash of vinegar to the cooking fat, and you'll enhance the flavor while reducing the tendency to stick.

■ If you like your poached or fried eggs neatly shaped, an empty tuna can with the ends cut out makes a fine egg holder.

Note: For hundreds more recipes and food tips, be sure to get a copy of *Wild Game Cookbook* from the Remington Sportsmen's Library. It offers good advice for the camper and outdoorsman.

53

Recreational Vehicle Camping

The commercially produced recreational vehicle ("rec vehicle" or simply "RV" in the current vernacular) is the realization of a dream that's been a long time in the making. There's nothing new, of course, in roaming about with some sort of wagon or cart in tow. What's different is that now the vagabonding is done for pleasure rather than of necessity.

But there is much more to roving with an RV than simply climbing aboard and accelerating down the blacktop. The novice rec-vehicle camper is well advised to do some thorough investigating of units at shows and dealer-display areas before buying, and the veteran enthusiast should keep up to date on rules and regulations, expanding his knowledge of safety practices as well as the technical aspects of his rig.

But, before you buy a recreational vehicle, consider renting a unit in the category that initially attracts your fancy. In capsule form, here are the major advantages and disadvantages of the basic RV types.

CAMPING TRAILERS

Camping trailers are the boxlike affairs that were once referred to as tent trailers. Very few now come with full soft tops and sides. At least one major maker is offering a unit that is hard-topped and solid-walled. Camping trailers, ranging from the tiny four-by-seven-foot models to the giant fourteen-foot units, can be the cheapest rec vehicle to buy and use. They are light, have a low center of gravity when folded for towing and preclude the need for big load-equalizing hitches or long-bracket mirrors. They handle the rough country well, too. And, of course, they can be unhitched when not in use. On the minus side, they're often chilly in cold weather, the whole unit must be opened to get at anything stored within and some of the bigger units can twist themselves out of alignment after a couple of years running on the rough.

TRAVEL TRAILERS

The most popular RV on the road—though camping trailers are close behind and gaining—travel trailers, too, permit you to unhitch the rig and drive around in your prime mover. When you return, you'll still have a camping spot. For practical towing, choose a unit no longer than twenty feet. These rec vehicles have high re-sale value because of their popularity.

They are very roomy inside and offer most of the comforts of home. They do require extended mirrors, load-equalizers and electric brakes, and they are not for backcountry exploration where roads or tracks are narrow. They are a bit of a chore for the novice to back around. Parking often becomes a problem.

TRUCK CAMPERS

Ranging from a pickup with a simple cover or shell to plush chassis-mounted cab-over coaches, truck campers offer more mobility than trailers for backcountry exploration. With these, you also have the option of towing a boat trailer. Your shelter rides on the same wheels as you do, which, some experts claim, gives a much better feel and control of the unit. If you have a shell unit or slide-in unit, you can dismount it and use the truck alone back home. But each time you're ready to move on, you have to pack up, stowing everything that might rattle while driving. In busy campgrounds, you may lose your site when leaving to explore— unless you remember to tote along a small pop-style tent to act as an "occupied" announcement.

MOTOR HOMES AND VANS

In the category of motor homes and vans, you can choose anything from a simple delivery-type wagon to a plush twenty-thousand-dollar wheeled land "yacht." Aside from affording a great degree of built-in comfort, the main attraction of these rigs is that the driver is not cut off from the living area as he is in a truck camper. The big units, however, don't maneuver well on narrow roads, and once a trip is over, they don't lend themselves well to around-town shopping.

Choosing the right RV for your personal needs can be a perplexing problem. If you're interested mainly in touring in comfort, the largest unit that lets you feel at ease while driving (and that you can afford) is the right choice. A person whose main aim is travel but who also dabbles in some outdoor sport would be wise to pick a medium-sized travel trailer, one of the larger camping trailers, one of the smaller motor homes or a well-equipped truck camper. The hard-core fishing-hunting outdoor family generally favors light camping trailers or travel trailers, the more rugged truck campers or occasionally a practical, not-too-fancy van in the smaller size.

■ When you decide on the type of unit you want, check the various makes with an eye toward basic overall practicality and quality of design and workmanship. How are the inside layouts for your particular needs? How tough is the roof and floor? You may very well need to haul extra gear on top, and when the rig is leveled with jacks while parked on uneven terrain, extra stress is placed on the floor.

■ When using an RV, many campers stretch the driving day, knowing that their modern units are ready for sleeping or cooking-eating use in minutes, as opposed to car camping wherein the tent must be hauled out and equipment unpacked and set up. Unfortunately, during the season's height, it's not so easy to find last-minute room at the local official campground. Stranded RV veterans have learned how to cope with this problem. They often utilize turnoffs and rest stops on major highways. In unpopulated areas, pulling off onto the road shoulder is fine—if it's permitted in the state you're in (check the department of highway safety in the states you'll be driving through). Some towns or cities will let you park overnight within the limits. Others levy big fines if you try it. Check with the police department. Within towns, the local park is sometimes open to RV tourists. Boatyards and factory and supermarket parking lots are other possibilities, but get permission first.

■ Take along a small extra tent when using a rec vehicle. You can use it to reserve your campsite, as an extra room for the kids or for storage.

■ Once you've parked—whether it's just for a night or longer—make sure your unit is level. You can affix one of the tape-on carpenter-type levels right to the RV, or you can use one of the genuine articles. If you don't have one, place a glass of water inside on a table or cabinet and see whether the waterline is parallel to the glass rim.

■ Use rubber chocks with tie-downs to hold them together and to both sides of each wheel when leaving a trailer parked—even on level ground. This is the surest blocking method yet.

■ Sponges with an adhesive strip placed on one side or two-sided plastic *foam* tape (with one side left covered) can be stuck just about anywhere as bumpers to eliminate nerve-racking rattles and bumps while you are under way.

■ The space between a camper coach and the truck carrying it is generally cool—a good place to store extra perishables. A small, inexpensive foam ice chest will work wonders inserted here. The ice will melt slowly because of the air flow created by traveling.

■ The most accurate device for measuring the amount of gas contained in a propane or butane tank is scales. Some gas dealers have no accurate scales, however, and then the measuring method is as

57

follows. The little tank valve (commonly known as a 10-percent valve) is left open. When it emits small spurts of vapor or white mist, the tank is filled enough. Overfilling results in the emitting of a steady vapor stream. If such is the case, drain off some of the gas.

■ Turnbuckles used to fasten some truck coaches to pickup beds or to hold camping trailer tops down can be made more effective by adding a safety nut to the hook threads, then putting on the buckle. Hand-tighten as usual, then run the nut up against the buckle. It works on the same principle as the second locking rings on many fishing-reel seats.

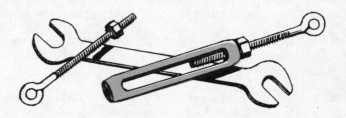

■ Without a gauge, the tea kettle test will provide a rough indication of how much liquid petroleum (LP) gas remains in your tank. Pour a little warm water from the tea kettle over the tank. Then feel the sides for the coldest area while checking for condensation. The level of cold or the condensation line that forms will be the level of the pressurized liquid inside the tank.

■ If your camping trailer has canvas sides, occasionally spray the zippers with one of the popular silicone lubricants. This will add life to the zippers without discoloring the canvas. When you must have new zippers installed, remember that those made of brass wear better than the aluminum variety.

■ Cracks that occur in the road cover of a camping trailer are easily repaired with fiberglass cloth and the appropriate resin. The repair is inexpensive to make and permanent.

■ The plywood underparts of RV tables and bunks will last longer if you give them a coat of good wood preservative.

■ It pays to understand some working differences between the two liquid petroleum (LP) gases—propane and butane—commonly used to fuel rec-vehicle appliances. Propane has a much greater vapor pressure (ninety-two pounds per square inch) than butane (only twelve pounds per square inch). Butane is not suited to temperatures below freezing. In many areas, blends of propane and butane are sold since such combinations can produce higher overall British thermal unit (Btu) ratings. Butane yields about 103,000 Btu's per gallon, propane about 91,500. If you are suddenly experiencing appliance trouble as the weather turns cool, suspect that your butane-propane mixture contains too much butane. Either cut back on the amount of butane in your fuel mixture or eliminate it entirely, using pure propane.

Because of the condensation that forms on LP gas-tank regulators, they can freeze in winter—particularly if the POL (petroleum, oil and lubricants) valve is left open on an empty tank. Unvaporized LP gas will not absorb much moisture (about one-tenth of an ounce in a hundred-pound tank), but vaporized gas holds ten times as much. Only a drop or two will freeze a regulator.

■ An LP gas tank filled with compressed air—140 to 150 pounds—is a handy thing to have when traveling the backcountry. You never can tell when you might need to use it to inflate a tire or jog dirt from a clogged fuel line. Standard pipe fittings, an air hose and a chuck will do for the conversion job. Keep the top valve closed tightly to prevent air leakage. Mount the tank so that it may be easily released from the holder for moving about on different jobs.

■ A simple drinking-cup holder for mounting on the inside of any RV can be built as follows. Construct a four-sided box large enough to accommodate the diameter of the cups you use and

high enough to handle the number you want to stack. The box should be closed at the bottom and open at the other end. A vertical slot is sawed down the length of one side, top to bottom, to permit the cup handles to stick out. Stack them upside down in the box. Cups are easily removed, one at a time, by grasping the protruding handle and sliding it up and out.

■ When choosing extension cords for electrical hookups, remember that the heavier the wire, the more effective use you'll be making of available power. Remember, too, that since all wires have a certain amount of power resistance (measured in ohms), the longer the wire between rec vehicle and hookup, the more resistance will be built up. Never use an indoor extension cord, with a seven-amp rating, for outdoor use. Twenty-five feet of number 12 three-wire extension cord will meet most RV requirements. For heavy-draw appliances, such as big heaters or air conditioners, fifty feet of number 10 three-wire cord is standard. It will handle about a twenty-five-amp load.

■ A mirror on a bracket, mounted high on the tongue of a heavy trailer and aimed down, will enable a lone driver to back his prime mover up to the hitch without having to jump in and out of the car or truck to check his positioning. The driver simply checks through his rear window to match up the tow vehicle's ball hitch or pintle with the tongue in one smooth operation.

If you are towing with a sedan or station wagon, you can make a handy gear-storage unit for it by using the principle of a cloth shoe-storage bag. Canvas or light tent poplin is sewn to drape over the front seat. Bags or compartments are sewn to the material hanging over the back. They will hold Thermos bottles, snacks, sunglasses and such easy-to-lose small items as bottle openers.

■ Beginning trailerists—whether towing a camping or a travel trailer—should know that the trailer wheels, when making turns, do not follow in the exact path of those of the tow vehicle. Make your turns wide so that the trailer wheels, which cut closer in the turn direction, will not bump curbs or other obstacles.

■ The best place to learn to back up a trailer is in a large empty parking lot, on a little-traveled road or in an open field. Remember that the wheels are turned in the opposite direction to those of a car. You may find it simplest, as many do, to grip the tow vehicle steering wheel at the bottom. Turn the wheel in the direction you want the trailer's rear end to go.

■ Brushing a soapy solution on valves and hose connections that are under high-LP pressure to find leaks has long been practiced by sportsmen using RV's and even by tent campers owning portable gas stoves. To locate even the tiniest of leaks, try painting connections with the concoction kids use to make bubbles. This solution will bubble up leaks missed by the standard soap-water mixture.

■ Here's a handy checklist for tuning up your RV rig each season *before* the first major trip.

Brakes: If you are going to tow a trailer large enough to require separate brakes, have the electrical magnets of the system checked. The trailer brakes should be tested alone for response and stopping power. Then adjust the manual control to the response setting you prefer.

Tires and wheels: Each should be checked for cracks, worn spots, chunking, separation. Inflate tires to proper pressure. Dig out any foreign objects lodged between treads. Have wheel bearings checked and repacked if necessary. Tighten all wheel nuts.

Hitch: For towed vehicles, check hitches for fatigue signs—especially at the joints. Ball hitches or pintles should be examined for cracks. All nuts should be tightened and threads should be cleaned of corrosion. Antisway devices must be adjusted per manufacturer's instructions.

Waterlines: All lines should have been emptied prior to cold weather. Sanitary systems ought to be flushed with water and possibly cleaning compounds that do not include harsh detergents. Holding tanks should be checked for dents that might later result in sudden leaks. Replace sludge-crusted drain hoses. Replace the water-purifier filter, close all drain plugs and fill water system after the tank has been cleaned of mineral and/or sand deposits.

Electrical system: Clean all corrosion from batteries. Have the battery tested and recharged if necessary. Worn-out fuses should be replaced. Make certain that breakaway switch is operating.

Miscellaneous: Nuts, brackets and bolts must be checked and tightened on such accessories as auxiliary gas tanks, bike racks, spare tires, sewer-hose connectors, license plates, awning brackets, locks, kitchen-cabinet handles, window hinges and hinged vents. In short, inspect anything and everything that could have vibrated loose over the past season.

Then have the motor end of your vehicle completely serviced by the best mechanic you can find.

■ Never store a camping trailer or travel trailer for the winter with the tires supporting the weight. Long periods of disuse will cause such load-supporting tires to develop flat spots. Although these may ride out, the overall tire structure will be weakened. The trailer should be jacked up, off the wheels. If space allows, remove the tires and wheels entirely, rope them through the rims and hang them on hooks out of the weather.

■ A simple heat deflector for LP-powered lamps will prevent trailer or coach ceilings from becoming discolored or blistered—and will help trap soot formed when burning in a new mantle. With a sheet-metal screw, just attach a spun-aluminum pie plate to the ceiling directly over the lamp—lip down toward the heat. Use this device even with lamps with built-in deflectors.

■ When gas lines are full of air, you are often forced to hold lighted matches until they burn your fingers to light stubborn pilots. To make a handy match holder that eliminates burned fingers, cut an eight- to twelve-inch length of wire clothes hanger and remove the finish from one end. Crimp an alligator clip (available from elec-

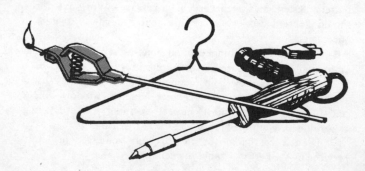

tronic-supply houses and some hardware stores) onto the bare metal end. Solder it down, using a good resin-core solder. The match is then placed in the teeth of the alligator clip. It's good for reaching hard-to-get-at furnace and water-heater pilots at home, too.

■ Tire change for a single-axle trailer is facilitated by placing the inflated spare on the ground and then driving up on it. This will give you more space beneath the frame for inserting the jack. The spare is pulled out, of course, and used as soon as the rig is jacked up. On dual-axle rigs, drive the inflated tire next to the flat up on a wood block or log (six to eight inches high). This will provide a good amount of extra elevation for removing the flat.

■ After you have unbolted a big, heavy RV tire, just pull from the bottom to remove it rather than horsing it. It should slide off easily. To remount a heavy tire and wheel, use the lug wrench as a lever. Lay the wrench on the ground in front of the axle, roll the spare onto it and then lift the end of the wrench closest to you. A shovel can serve the same purpose.

■ Heavy steel axle skids used on trailers and other rec vehicles are not only effective safety devices but they also save on tire and chassis damage in case of blowouts. Set at a level to come in contact with the ground before the tire loses all its air, they are most valuable on rigs with single axles.

■ Don't be misled by coach-truck weight recommendations when assembling a truck-camper package. Many coach bodies that are rated for, say, a three-quarter-ton truck should actually be used on nothing smaller than a one-ton pickup. Stripped of extras, the coach body in question could conceivably be handled by a three-quarter-ton prime mover that was also sparse in the accessory department. Add full water tanks, holding tanks, people, camping equipment, radio, power steering, air conditioning and you have an unsafe rig. The key figure to consider is the truck's gross vehicle weight (GVW)—the total weight the truck is designed to carry, *including* its own weight. Figure the weight of the various items you plan to install in your truck-camper package as closely as possible, leaving room for a little extra. Then decide what coach-and-truck combination will be best for you.

■ The number of motor campers buying four-wheel-drive vehicles is on the upswing. Unfortunately, novices to this sort of driving frequently make the mistake of leaping into their brand-new chariots and heading to the backcountry in glazed-eye ecstasy with never a thought to emergency equipment. Many of them rue their heedlessness when they find out about wallet-gouging tow-out fees or long, lonely hikes back to civilization. Learn to prepare for the unexpected by toting at least the following emergency items:

> **Aluminum survival blanket**
> **Chains**
> **Come-along (pulley rig)**
> **Electrician's tape**
> **Engine oil (at least two quarts)**
> **Fan belt**
> **Flares**
> **Flashlight**
> **Food rations**
> **Fuses**
> **Gasoline (five gallons extra)**
> **Glue (epoxy)**
> **Jacks (high-lift type and an axle jack)**
> **Jumper cables**
> **Matches (waterproof)**
> **Permatex (self-hardening and nonhardening sealant)**
> **Pump (spark-plug type is good)**
> **Shovel**
> **Spark plugs**
> **Tow strap or chain**
> **Wire (bailing)**
> **Wood (three-quarter-inch plywood to place jacks upon)**

During the winter or when heading into the mountains where snow may still be present, be sure to take along a shovel and sand or a short strip of wire grating to provide traction in case your vehicle gets stuck.

■ Taking your dog along on a major trip can be very rewarding and will not present many problems if you plan ahead. Most canines delight in the sights, sounds and odors of new places. Some of them, though, do not take to the actual traveling. You should already have some idea of your dog's reaction to short trips, so that you can be prepared. Extremely active dogs or undisciplined ones may do very well in one of the cage carriers used for transporting hunting dogs. Realizing their confinement, most dogs will quickly settle down in such carriers. You can also keep the dog on a short check leash. This should work well, too, but it will keep one passenger occupied.

Never leave a dog tied by his leash without someone nearby to watch him. Too many dogs have choked themselves by leaping after other animals, trying to get free or just getting tangled in their leashes. Always leave a window open to give your pet adequate ventilation.

Unless you are very certain of your animal's trustworthiness, don't leave him in a closed coach to which you have no direct access while driving. You may discover your dream rig's interior chewed to splinters when you stop.

Carry a good supply of water with you and offer your dog a drink at each stop. Make a few special stops just for him. Feeding is often not advised during short rest stops because an excited dog may gobble quickly and become ill when he is back in the vehicle.

Always keep your dog on a leash during stops at strange areas; otherwise, he may bolt.

Do not let your dog ride with his head outside a window. It is not good for his eyes or ears and can be distracting to other motorists.

■ Two locales—deserts and mountains—call for special driving techniques. Always check your cooling system before heading out into a desert or mountains. Bring extra water—the collapsible plastic containers sold in many camp-supply stores are ideal for this. Do not drive fast in deserts or you may have an overheating problem. Use your air-conditioning sparingly. If your vehicle begins overheating to an extreme degree, stop. Let the engine cool before opening the radiator cap to add more water. Drink some water yourself while waiting. You need much more than you normally would.

In mountains, sound your horn when approaching blind turns and hold closely to your side of the road—especially if you are driving a large camping vehicle. Never stop on narrow mountain roads to photograph or sightsee. Use gearing and resultant motor drag to aid you in descents—this includes rigs with automatic transmissions. Steady braking may cause fade, and if you brake suddenly, too hard, you could put your vehicle into a skid. If your engine becomes overheated from a long climb, vapor lock may occur. This is nothing more than the fuel vaporizing in the lines. In vapor form, it blocks the line and the engine will fail to give full power. It may idle poorly or stall, and it may fail to restart. Open the hood, wait ten to fifteen minutes and you should be able to start again.

Canoeing
and
Boating

Canoes, rowboats, outboard-driven runabouts, sailboats, houseboats, inboard-driven racers, sportfishermen—an astounding variety and number of vessels dot the coastal marinas and inland waterways. Obviously, no one has to be sold on the pleasures of boating or on the fact that a knowledge of techniques and equipment will enhance those pleasures. But accident statistics show that far too many of us still have to be sold on the importance of knowing and following safety rules.

The first rule is that powerboats must give a wide berth to craft relying on oars, paddles or sails. A powerboat's wake can stop or sometimes even capsize a smaller, less stable and less maneuverable vessel.

Second, for the same reason, all boats without power have the right of way over powerboats.

Third, if you find yourself and another skipper closing head on, steer to the right. The other skipper will do the same. All boats, then, should steer to starboard and pass each other portside to portside. Always slow down when passing close. To alert the other vessel that you are about to pass, a powerboat should be equipped with a whistle or horn to blow one short blast; the reply is also one short blast.

If two vessels are on a collision course more or less at right angles, the boat on the right-hand side is "privileged"—it has the right of way. The other is "burdened" and must slow down or alter course. In other words, if a boat is approaching your starboard bow, danger exists and you must give way.

An overtaken boat that is headed in the same direction retains the right of way; the passing one must keep clear.

Craft leaving docks are considered burdened and must watch for those in the waterway before moving out into traffic. Craft approaching an anchorage or dock must throttle down to avoid making a heavy wake that might damage tied boats.

As with other outdoor pursuits, procedures for boating are simple once you know them, and they're mostly based on common sense and thoughtfulness.

■ The secret of correct canoe loading is balance. Under normal conditions, place packs and as much other gear as possible at the center, keeping the bow and stern light. This will help to keep the craft stable and to make paddling easier. However, when going downstream in rough or rocky water, you can ride the current better by loading the canoe so that it's slightly bow-heavy. When poling or paddling upstream in this kind of water, make it slightly

67

stern-heavy to keep the bow high for easy sliding off submerged rocks.

■ If you're about to buy your first sailboat, bear in mind that a sailing craft with a pivoting centerboard can negotiate shallow waters more easily than a boat with a deep, immovable iron or lead keel.

■ If a gasoline motor's spark plugs are positioned horizontally, the plugs can be marked on the outside to make sure they are turned to keep the grounded electrodes pointing upward. A simple file mark will do. If necessary, put an extra gasket on the plugs so that they will have the mark upward when tightened. With this positioning, any oil or gas that gets on a plug will run down to its shell rather than into the gap and down to the center electrode to short it out.

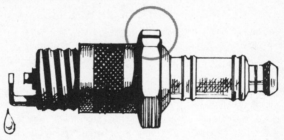

■ If your boat is a cartopper, the ropes running from bow and stern to your auto bumpers may rub paint off your car. To prevent this, wrap foam-rubber strips around the rope where it touches the car. Hold the rubber in place by wrapping it with plastic tape at two or three spots.

■ Don't begin a long canoe trip without a repair kit, available at boating-goods stores. To repair a canvas canoe, you'll need ambroid glue, unbleached muslin patches and sandpaper to roughen the edges and give the glue a firm bond. For an aluminum canoe, all you need is a tube of liquid solder and possibly one or two small aluminum patches. For a fiberglass canoe, you'll need epoxy-resin glue and hardener.

■ Having trouble launching from a trailer? A ball hitch installed on your car's front bumper will allow you to push the trailer to the water, with the car going forward instead of in reverse. When you arrive at the ramp, unhitch the trailer from its normal position at the back of the car, turn the car around and attach the trailer hitch to the front bumper ball. You can then drive straight ahead to push the trailer down the ramp to the water. With the trailer still in this front position, you can later pick up the boat again, then turn the car around and rehitch in the normal manner.

■ When rowing at night, keeping the oar blades at the proper angle is difficult except for those that are held in position by an oarlock pin—they can't be feathered. The problem can be solved by cutting or rasping the oar grips to a slightly oval shape, with the long sides of the oval at right angles to the blade. Then sand the grips smooth. Your hands will be able to feel the oval and thereby choose the proper blade angle in the dark.

■ Motorists will seldom begin a trip without a spare tire, but those who trailer their boats often neglect to take along a spare trailer tire. It is also wise to check the trailer's tire pressure frequently because unequal pressure can cause whipping from side to side. And be sure to have a wrench that fits the trailer-wheel lugs, plus a jack that can get a firm purchase on the trailer. A small scissors-type jack, costing less than ten dollars, can easily lift three thousand pounds. A hydraulic jack is needed for bigger loads.

■ Floating rope (polyethylene or polypropylene) is good for anchor line. It's strong and flexible, and if you ever forget to tie the end to the boat, you won't lose it and the anchor when you throw the anchor over. All you have to do to retrieve the anchor is lift the floating end of the rope from the water.

■ Since sheets (the lines used to trim the sails on a sailboat) and halyards (the vertical lines used to hoist the sails) are the key to sailing control, this running rigging should be inspected for wear—regularly and rigorously. The actual reeving (rigging of the sheets through the blocks) should be done very methodically and carefully until the procedure with your particular boat has become so routine that you know you could do it blindfolded. Halyards will inevitably intertwine, sometimes snarling so badly that sails will not go up or down; your major concern with the halyards is to keep them clear, always untangling them before raising sail.

■ A flotation boat cushion won't do you much good if it's out of reach when you hit the water. A dog leash or a four-foot length of clothesline with a ring on one end and a snap on the other will keep the cushion at heel. Just pass one end through the cushion's loop and snap the other to your belt or belt loop.

■ To prevent losing your boat keys if they fall into the water, run the key chain through a hook eye and screw a cork onto the eye.

■ A woven plastic or wire bike basket is a handy carryall for first-aid kit, camera, snacks, etc., and the curved hangers will fit nicely over a small boat's gunnel so that the basket is mounted right at your fingertips.

■ A plastic food container or refrigerator dish with an airtight snap-on cover makes a fine "valuables safe" for a boat or canoe. It will keep your watch or billfold dry, and it will float in the event of a mishap.

■ To make a cheap, durable, quiet anchor that won't mar a boat or canoe, fill a gallon plastic bleach bottle with sand or concrete mix. Just screw the cap back on and attach the anchor rope through the jug's handle.

■ Another useful plastic container is a prescription bottle of the right size to hold wooden matches. It's waterproof and it will float.

■ Larger plastic bottles have yet another use. Freeze water in them, and they'll keep your ice chest cold. Later, when the water in them has melted sufficiently, you'll have ice water to drink.

■ For safety's sake, the most important of all boating items is a flotation vest or jacket, but merely wearing one is not full insurance against disaster if a boat capsizes far from shore. Swimming away can be a fatal mistake because of the dangers of cramps, fatigue and exposure to cold water. Since modern boats are virtually unsinkable, it makes sense to stay with the craft and hold onto it to save your strength. Unless your boat is very small, you can usually climb right up on the overturned hull and rest there until rescue arrives. Besides, a capsized or swamped boat will eventually drift in toward shore. Do not thrash around in the water trying to salvage cushions, floorboards or even expensive fishing tackle—none of it is as valuable as your life.

■ A light canoe that capsizes can often be pushed to shallow water by a strong swimmer; it is then reasonably easy to turn the craft upright, reboard it and start bailing. However, righting a canoe in deep water can be dangerous (and sometimes impossible) for anyone but an expert. With the exception of centerboard-equipped sailboats, it is futile and hazardous to try to right any heavy vessel while you are swimming in deep water.

■ Sailboats capsize more frequently than other vessels. When such a boat begins to tip, the crew should immediately let out the sails and climb to the high side. Even if these measures fail to prevent the boat from capsizing, they will keep you out from under mainsail and mast. A small centerboard sailboat can often be righted. Be sure the centerboard is fully extended through its trunk. If possible, slacken sheets and halyards, haul in sails and put the anchor out to windward to keep the craft headed into the wind. The crew then stands on the centerboard, gripping the coaming and leaning back. For still more leverage, one man can pull on a line looped around the shrouds. All of this is difficult and risks damaging the boat; unless the craft is small, the crew skilled and the chance of success good, a tow to shallow water is recommended.

■ Powerboat skippers should use extreme caution when coming to the aid of a capsized boat. Approach slowly, watching carefully for people and objects in the water. A capsized boat should be towed at a very low speed to prevent hull damage.

■ To make an aluminum canoe slide over rocks more easily, you need only to wax the bottom.

■ For nighttime boating or sailing, you should be thoroughly familiar with the U.S. navigational system, which uses red, green and white lights to mark obstructions and channels. White, used only because it shows up well in the dark, is found in combination with red or green. Green lights (marked *G* on the charts) indicate boundaries on the port side and red (*R* on the charts) show starboard boundaries. The skipper must therefore steer to keep the green lights to port, the red to starboard, on entering harbors. Quick-flashing lights (one flash per second or faster) in either color tell you to observe special caution. And you should need no reminder to maintain your own proper running lights in perfect condition.

■ When storing an outboard motor, cover it with an old sheet or other large cloth to keep dust out. Don't use an airtight covering, such as plastic sheeting, because it will hold in moisture instead of protecting the motor.

■ Never simply pour gasoline and oil into an outboard tank, guessing at the proportions. Use a five- or six-gallon container to mix exactly the ratio recommended for your motor, and you'll find that it starts more easily and runs more smoothly.

■ A piece of aluminum foil wrapped around an oar will stay in place temporarily and stop the oar from squeaking in the lock. A thick leather wrapping, cemented and nailed, can later be used as a more permanent remedy.

■ Soap will seal a small gas-line leak temporarily.

■ When buying an outboard motor, remember that great horsepower is not usually needed (or sometimes even desirable) on the smaller waterways. Outboards are lighter than ever before, but anything over five horsepower is still likely to weigh more than forty pounds. The woman of the family will have trouble lugging such a motor, and even a strong man won't enjoy toting it about. Also, the smaller a motor is, the easier it is to store or cram into a car trunk or the back of a packed station wagon. If you do need more than five horsepower, bear in mind that some manufacturers now offer motors of just under ten horsepower, which is the wisest choice for many waters. Some states and Canadian provinces require you to register any boat equipped with a motor of ten horsepower or more. This is fine when you reside in that state or province and use the motor on only your own boat. Otherwise, it can be a problem. Motors just under ten horsepower usually require no registration.

■ On a canoe trip in unfamiliar country, cross each portage first with your pack, not with the canoe. The average portage is an obstacle course that should be studied before you attempt to get the craft over it.

■ Here is a choice of ways to solve the broken shear-pin problem. Keep spare shear pins in a thirty-five-millimeter film container. Or tape a spare, together with a cotter key, to the handle of your outboard motor. Or tape several pins and keys, plus small pliers, to the motor and you'll have no trouble at all changing a broken pin on the spot. Or, if you've broken pin after pin and are getting discouraged about keeping spares on hand, a welding-supply company can furnish a length of brazing or soft welding rod of the same diameter as your shear pin. Tape it to a safe place inside your boat and snip off the right length when you need it.

■ Electric outboards are primarily for fishing, of course, and aren't intended to provide much power or speed, but most models can be mounted anywhere along the gunnel and can give you excellent maneuverability even in wind. For proper control, however, there are tricks to using such a motor. To buck a light breeze, leave the motor mounted on the transom in the normal manner but put it in reverse and proceed stern first. For a heavier blow, move the motor up near the bow, point the bow into the wind and let the motor (now in forward gear rather than reverse) pull the boat instead of pushing it. You can then maintain good control, speeding up to make progress upwind, slowing down to drift downwind.

■ For all-around use, the ideal canoe is generally considered to be a flat-bottomed model about seventeen feet long, three feet wide at the center and a little over a foot deep. Don't get a square-ender unless you intend to use a motor.

■ When you are paddling alone, your canoe will balance best if you kneel or sit at the center facing the bow or at the bow facing the stern. When two people are canoeing, the more experienced paddler should be at the stern so that he can steer and also keep an eye on the load and make minor corrections for the bow paddler.

■ Here's how to choose a canoe paddle. When you stand straight and hold a stern paddle upright with its blade touching the ground, it should reach to about eye level or just below. A bow paddle should come to your chin or just below. The best paddles are made of white ash, which has the right weight and springiness. Other good woods are white spruce and hard maple.

■ The J-stroke in paddling is inefficient but is the easiest technique for novices. Hold your arms fairly straight as the paddle goes into the water, with the blade close to the canoe. Sweep the paddle rearward, and at the end of the stroke, move it outward and slightly forward, completing the J as you feather it up out of the water. With practice, this can be modified into the far more efficient pitch stroke, or guide stroke, which prevents zigzagging. The paddle goes straight back, without the hook that forms the J-sweep, while you turn the blade at a gradually increasing angle until you finally move it slightly outward and feather it at the end of the stroke.

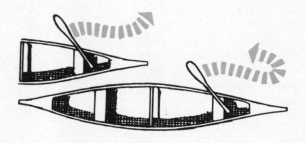

■ In small boats, a fine piece of equipment to have is a one- or two-burner Sterno stove. When the day is chilly or damp, the little stove is great for making hot soup, coffee, tea or a couple of fried eggs and bacon.

■ On sailing vessels, the skipper would be well advised to carry a sheath knife on his belt in case an emergency arises requiring rigging to be cut immediately.

■ The Beaufort scale is a traditional wind-estimation guide based on wave action. The higher the scale number, the rougher the water and the stiffer the wind. For example, force 8 is a fresh gale, force 9 is a strong gale, force 10 is a whole gale (wind velocity of forty-eight to fifty-five knots), force 11 is a storm and force 12 is a hurricane (above sixty-six knots). Although the lowest forces on the scale have little effect on engine- or motor-driven craft, familiarity with them is advisable for all boatmen and essential for sailing enthusiasts. No small craft should be out at sea in anything as strong as a force 7 gale. The scale printed below is a sailing guide to forces from 1 through 7.

Wind Forces	Action of Sailboat	Water Conditions	Wind	Wind Velocity
1	Steerage way	Ripples	Light air	1-3 Knots
2	Sails fill	Small wavelets	Light breeze	4-6 Knots
3	Slight heel	Wavelets crest	Gentle breeze	7-10 Knots
4	Good heel	Small waves	Moderate breeze	11-16 Knots
5	First reef	Moderate waves	Fresh breeze	17-21 Knots
6	Double reef	Many whitecaps	Strong breeze	22-27 Knots
7	Hove to	Foam flies	Moderate gale	28-33 Knots

Saltwater Fishing

There's a popular belief that saltwater fishing is a snap. Although it is true that anglers occasionally stumble upon feeding frenzies of schooled fish, automatic success is not the rule. In fact, angling in the salt can be as demanding as freshwater sport.

■ Do-it-yourself billfishing is growing in popularity. It's cheaper than hiring a charter, and it permits the use of privately owned smaller boats. Timing is of great importance here. The owner of a smaller craft must keep tabs on fish migrations and local school movements. He has to be ready to move out at a moment's notice when sailfish, marlin or swordfish are in close enough for him to get action. Obviously, he cannot fish as far offshore as the big boats. Here are some techniques proved successful by the "mosquito" fleet of small sport craft.

Instead of trolling with the usual wooden teaser in conjunction with sewn natural baits, try rigging a large tandem "troll" with keel and several flashy spinners in front of the sewn bait. This gives the impression that the baitfish is chasing a school of small fry. To add an extra touch, employ a flashy saltwater spoon on a second rod. Troll this about fifteen feet behind the baitfish. A third rod can troll another spoon about twenty-five feet ahead of the baitfish for those gamesters lured in by prop vibration. You can add weight to these lures as situations dictate.

■ In rough water it is next to useless to fish for big game on the surface. Try using good live baitfish with a light-tackle setup. With a bait-sewing needle, stitch four or five loops of thread along the backs of live two-pound baitfish in front of the dorsal. If you do this carefully and then keep the baitfish in a live well, they'll be in good condition when you reach the fishing grounds. Then thread a 9/0 hook (short shank) through the loops and toss the live bait overboard to run where it will while you drift. Except for the sewing on

of loops, this is basically the same method used by freshwater fishermen. Not often used by the saltwater boys, but it works wonders.

■ When you can't spot billfish on the surface, use a method incorporating dead bait—fish or, preferably, squid. Sew on the bait and simply lower it while the boat drifts. The key to success here is having a partner who will pull off line to allow the bait to drift completely dead, with no hint of motion from the boat. The method is, of course, used in areas where bills have quite recently been sighted.

■ When shore fishing or angling from a boat close to shore in hot weather, fish the incoming tides. Game fish will come in with the cooler water and ease out with the ebbing tide ahead of the warm water.

■ You can cast all day to tarpon that are rolling on their sides and it is very doubtful that you'll get a strike. When the big silvers are going through these motions, it indicates they'll soon be sounding. Go to a bucktail or feathered lead jig and work the bottom.

■ It is often recommended to fasten plastic bags around reels left set up on matching rods. This is a good method for keeping dirt or dust out of your reel mechanism while transporting equipment in truck or car, but do not make a habit of leaving bags over reels that have been used all day long. The bags will hold moisture collected by the particles of salt still on the reel. Excessive moisture causes corrosion to begin and also results in earlier decomposition of line. It is better to install some sort of overhead holders from which to hang rods where air circulates freely.

■ When shore casting in a new area, wait for low tide, climb a dune, jetty or any other elevated point of land and scout the water with Polaroid sunglasses. You'll be able to see channels through which fish pass in and out with the tide. Also look for the big weed beds, mussel beds and large rocks that attract fish. Then do your fishing two hours before to two hours after high tide.

■ When fishing from piers or jetties, break up the mussels and barnacles that cling to these structures and toss them into the water to act as an on-the-spot natural chum.

■ Always use a plastic, fiberglass or wood tacklebox on saltwater trips. Aluminum and steel are subject to corrosion and rust and will last through only one or two seasons.

■ Bluefish, mackerel, yellowtail, albacore and other high-oil-content fish will spoil quickly if not treated properly from the moment they are boated. Plenty of ice should be at hand. Use broken-up ice rather than very heavy blocks that might bruise the flesh. When stowing fish in a tub or can, raise them off the bottom by any means available so that melting ice will not keep them soaking. Otherwise they may get soggy. Clean them as soon as possible.

■ Have trouble tying blood knots in heavy saltwater monofilament? Here's a trick that will make it easier, especially when the weather's cold enough to make knot-tying awkward. Wind the two ends five turns around each other in the usual manner. Then, instead of trying to work each end separately down through the middle loop, tie them together (any knot will do) first. You next jam this two-end knot through the loop in the usual way. No worry about one side springing out of your grasp and completely unwinding. Allow extra lengths of line so that you'll have enough left to tie the end knot.

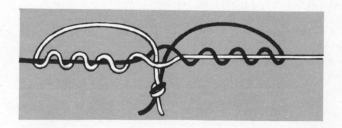

■ Clinch knots and improved clinch knots are standard with fresh-water fishermen using light leaders. Heavy leader used in the salt demands a different knot. The double turle does the job. To tie it, pass the leader through the hook eye from the front and slide the lure or hook up the leader out of the way. Make a simple overhand slipknot in the leader by bringing the end around *twice* over the standing leader. Draw the knot tight. Slide the lure back down the leader, bringing the slip loop over it from the rear. Pull the loop closed around the head of a fly or just behind a hook eye or plug eye, and you're in business.

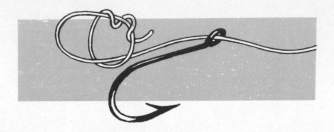

■ One more knot to add to your collection is the nail-knot *loop*. Based on the regular nail knot, it is often used for big-game fishing because tight knots made with heavy 80- to 100-pound mono around the eye of a fly or the head of a lure often kill the action of same. If you're using a shock tippet of such heavy mono, the nail-knot loop solves the problem. Thread the lure on the leader. Then bend the leader around the head of a three-and-a-half- or four-inch carpenter's nail, letting the lure hang at the bend. With the end of the leader, make three turns around the standing part and the nail from the nail point back toward the nail head, which should still be in place at the leader bend. Next draw the working end of the leader through the center of the turns from the bend toward the nail point. Let the nail drop free, hold one finger at the loop just ahead of the lure and pull the end of the leader with a small pair of pliers to tighten the turns into a solid knot. The lure will swing free on a loop which will not jam up against the eye until a very strong fish is hooked and fought.

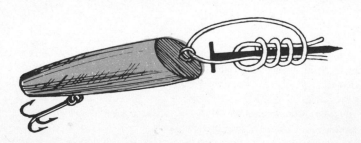

■ Many experts swear by bait for summer flounder—fluke, that is—whereas others prefer lures, including bucktail jigs, metal squid, hooks and pork rind. For the best of both worlds, try using a three-way swivel. The main line or leader is tied to one swivel eye. A sinker attached to lighter line than the leader is tied into the second swivel eye. Make the sinker line about six inches long. Tie a hook onto eight inches of leader from the third swivel eye. On it, attach a strip of white or yellow pork rind. Then impale a live killie, sand eel or dead spearing on the hook, through the head or through the lips. The result is a bait scent plus a slinky artificial attention-getter.

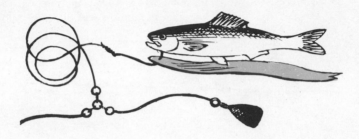

■ Striped bass are one of the more difficult sport fish to catch. They're temperamental, sometimes changing their feeding desires from day to day. There are many ways of fishing for stripers, but first you must know where to find them. Small school stripers generally frequent inlets or rivers. Fish for these around bridge supports, piers and breakwaters. Surf casters reach for the big fish around the inner edges of sandbars, rocks, deep holes and around rough water. Of course, boatmen make good use of bird-watching, charging to areas where gulls or terns are diving on baitfish driven up by schools of striped bass beneath them. (The same bird-watching trick also works when prospecting for bluefish.)

■ Striped-bass fishing is best on cloudy or drizzly days. Best times are early morning and evening, but the biggest bass are caught at night.

■ One of the truly effective baits for catching sheer numbers of striped bass is freshly killed menhaden. You can catch these oily baitfish yourself by snagging through a school—if the water is clear enough and calm enough to permit you to locate schools on the top. Otherwise, you can buy them. The bait must be fresh and kept so by stowing it on ice, in layers, in an inexpensive cooler. Use a strong seven- or eight-foot casting rod that can handle the two-pound menhaden in a cast. A conventional surf-casting reel is best. Rig up with mono in the forty-pound class. A large snap swivel is fixed to the end of the line. Attach a sinker (a drail or keel sinker is good) weighing from one to four ounces (depending on the current) to the snap. Tie a four-foot leader to the eyelet on the opposite end of the sinker. A 5/0 treble hook is attached to the end of the leader. Hook the menhaden from the bottom, up through the lips. Cast as close as possible to shore, jetties, etc., where fish are known to be. Or run your boat out and allow the bait to drift or slowly work it in with occasional twitches from the rod. Hits are felt as steady taps. Allow the bass to take the bait on a run before striking.

■ When trolling with cut strip baits, prevent the bait from riding up the leader by cutting two small disks from an old inner tube or other piece of rubber. Each disk should be no more than half an inch in diameter. Slit the center of each disk so that it will slip onto the hook. Then simply run one up the shank of the hook, leaving it below the eye. The other should be placed just above the hook barb.

■ Bluefishing in a chum slick can be quite productive. At times the fish will go wild, slashing and snapping at everything that seems edible and sometimes at things that aren't. This explains how blues earned the nickname "choppers." Blues will tear through a slick or school of baitfish just for the sheer pleasure of ripping things up. But even when they're in this sharklike frenzy, you must fish the slick by allowing your chunks of bait to drift with the tide and current. This means you must constantly spool out line by hand. Moving the bait away from the natural drift with your rod or holding it still against a strong current will spook the choppers. Let out a good amount of line and then reel in and start over again. Strike the moment you feel the slightest hit.

■ First-timers on bluefish must remember to keep their fingers away from the mouth of a blue that's just been brought into the boat. Everyone knows about the dangers of shark and barracuda teeth, but many anglers are unaware that a chopper's jaws can slice a finger down to the bone—or worse.

■ Another fish that can cause a terrific slash in your anatomy is the snook. The edges of his gill covers are so sharp that they can slice a line that moves over them as well as a hand.

■ Spoons, wobblers or spinners can put a nasty twist in your trolling line even when you use a swivel. But you can reduce, if not completely eliminate, this problem. Different lures rotate in different directions. Troll your hardware alongside the boat for a few moments to check its direction of rotation. Choose one, when you change lures, that rotates in the opposite direction. Planing keels or keel sinkers rigged ahead of the lure are even more effective in reducing twist. On your way back from a day's trolling, drag your line—sans lures—behind the boat.

■ Contrary to modern belief, the original fish-finder was not a portable sonar device. The fish-finder familiar to old-time saltwater buffs and used on a variety of species from speedy game fish to slow-moving bottom feeders is an integral part of the terminal rig. It can be employed by surf casters or boat fishermen. It is a slide arrangement that permits a baited hook with a sinker to be cast as a unit. After the bait is on the bottom, it is possible to feed line so that the hook can float with the tide away from the sinker, up and down depending on the direction of vagrant currents. One way of rigging this fish-finder is to attach a fairly large-eyed barrel swivel ahead of the hook (on the leader). Ahead of this swivel you thread the leader through the eye of a *snap* swivel (or leather or plastic slide made for the purpose). The eye on the snap swivel must not be able to travel over the first swivel on down to the hook. A bank or pyramid sinker is clipped into the snap. The remaining leader and the line can now run freely through the sinker's snap swivel, permitting the baited hook to drift as it will. An alternative arrangement involves tying in a cork bobber between the hook and the first swivel.

83

This will elevate the baited hook as it moves away from the weighted snap swivel.

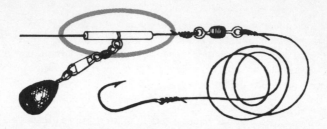

■ Fly rodders interested in trying the "long wand" in salt water need not plunk down a lot of loot for a new outfit before they are sure they're going to like the sport. If a rod will handle a weight-forward 7, 8, 9 or 10 line, you can use it for salt water. Make sure, though, that your reel will hold at least 100 yards of small-diameter Dacron backing.

■ Another tip for saltwater fly fishermen—also applicable to freshwater fishermen—involves the connection of the leader to the fly line. After the leader has been firmly affixed to the line with a nail knot, coat the knot with Plyobond cement. Let one coat dry; then apply a second layer. Wear caused by rubbing through the guides and tip top will be greatly reduced.

■ To join two sections of monofilament with widely varying diameters, as necessary when using a shock tippet, utilize the Stu Apte Improved Blood Knot. This is tied as the regular blood knot, described in just about every basic fishing book, but the smaller-diameter mono is doubled.

■ Sometimes when you are trolling for a billfish, he will knock the line free of the outrigger but fail to take the bait. In this case, the accepted procedure is to let the reel remain in free spool. Although it is true that in such situations a fish generally needs time to wheel around and find the bait, many anglers remain in free spool far too long, allowing the bait to drift away, which, naturally, loses the fish's attention. Try throwing the reel in gear and reeling suddenly. Try to anticipate a strike, just before the bait reaches the surface, by lowering your rod tip.

■ Most large saltwater fish love squid. When you can't obtain the real thing, the soft plastic imitation squid are excellent. To rig one, fix a cigar-shaped trolling lead ahead of the lure. In blue water you can troll the rig, allowing occasional drop-back. Inshore, over reefs, in rocky areas, try jigging the artificial lure, bouncing it off the bottom.

■ There will never be one all-purpose rod for all saltwater fishing. But for the new fisherman who is willing to forgo fishing in crowded party-boat situations and trolling for giant fish, an eight-and-a-half- to nine-foot spin stick is hard to beat. Choose an open-faced spinning reel with a big crank handle and the capacity to hold 300 yards of fifteen-pound monofilament.

■ Handy boat-rod holders can be made from sections of rubber hosing bracketed to the gunwales or to plywood boards which are in turn hinged to the gunwales, using a removable pin so that the whole works can be removed when not needed. Plastic piping works, too, and it's usually easier to obtain in large diameter than the rubber.

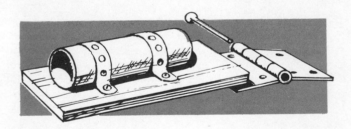

■ A handy boat plug-and-lure holder to supplement overflowing tackle boxes can be made by cutting a sheet of three-eighths-inch marine plywood about fifteen by twelve inches. Using a hole saw, make about forty circles in the wood large enough to hold the small plastic drinking cups generally used for fruit juice. Make two sides of one-inch pine, each twelve inches long. After the sides have been brass-screwed to the top, you will have a tablelike arrangement. Insert the cups into the holes and glue them to the sides with waterproof adhesive. When dry, punch holes in the cup bottoms for drainage. You can then cut rubber to fit each corner of the underside and glue it down to prevent the rig from slipping on slick surfaces. A lure is plopped into each cup.

■ It is far better to have only a few types of plugs in a wide range of colors than a great variety of plugs of different makes. Basically, plugs can wiggle either sideways or up and down. Stick to a few of the best-known, time-proved plugs of reputable make and concentrate on stocking every hue available.

■ Eels, dead or alive, are fine bait for many game species. They are especially favored by striped bass and bluefish. Almost all saltwater creeks that empty into bays, sounds or tidal rivers have a good supply of eels. An inexpensive minnow trap is ideal for catching them in the six- to fifteen-inch size—the best size for bait. Bait the trap with crushed clams, mussels or fish scraps. If you like to eat eels, too, you can use an eelpot but you'll then have to sort the bait size from the larger variety. Since eels will keep well for months even in fresh water, you can maintain a supply—still in the trap—in a backyard pond or nearby stream.

■ Eels are squirmy and difficult to hook. An old burlap sack held in one hand will permit you to grasp the eel for baiting through the lips from below. Another trick is to keep a bucket of sand on your boat. Wet your hand and dip it in the sand before grasping the eel firmly. Toss hooked eels overboard quickly before they have a chance to turn the leader and line into a nightmarish tangle. (In the water they tend to swim freely without twisting.) You can also tail-hook an eel. He'll tend to tangle even less this way, but you won't be able to retrieve the bait without drowning it. The head will appear swollen when this has happened.

■ Adjust the running action on floating and sinking plugs as follows. Bend the front eyelet up to decrease the action speed; bend it down to increase the action. For side-to-side adjustment—used when a plug is running with one side down—bend the leader eyelet toward the side which is running low. This side-to-side adjustment works for deep-running plugs, too. Use small pliers and make only minor adjustments at a time, testing the lure after each alteration.

■ All kinds of shrimp, especially the tiny grass shrimp, are ideal baits for the smaller inshore saltwater gamesters, for big bass that sometimes forage close to the beaches and for such freshwater fish as trout. To capture grass shrimp, wade along tidal grasslands near rivers or on bays. Where the grass-covered banks meet the water edge, work a small hand-held bait net up under the banks where the roots hang down. You'll scrape up any number of the translucent little fellows this way—at least in areas that have not been hit with sprays for mosquito control. Keep the shrimp alive between layers of wet seaweed or in damp sawdust. They'll die in unaerated water buckets.

■ It is possible to take winter-run whiting on saltwater fly rods. These tasty northeastern fish can be hooked on all kinds of bait, but fly rodders who have experimented have found that they can cash in on the "frosty" runs, too. They choose weather conditions that drive baitfish in close to jetty or beach. They also keep a lantern going near the water to help attract the baitfish. With a beefy rod and a white chenille or silver Mylar fly tied with marabou blood feathers, it's not hard to score—if you can take the chill December weather.

■ A good way to cover vast areas of ocean while searching for schools of fish is to troll with jigs. The lead-head jigs with interchangeable plastic tails work well. Try different trolling speeds, and make sure your jig is heavy enough to reach bottom. When using jigs, however, remember that the angler must supply the action. Make sharp twitching motions with the rod, not huge sweeps, while trolling. If your rod is soft in the tip, you will not get the proper action.

■ In the East, flounder fishermen make good use of fresh-frozen corn kernels for chumming and as bait on the hook. Not to be outdone, surfmen in California go for opaleye with moss (these fish are algae grazers), and they catch surf perch with fresh-frozen peas.

Freshwater Fishing

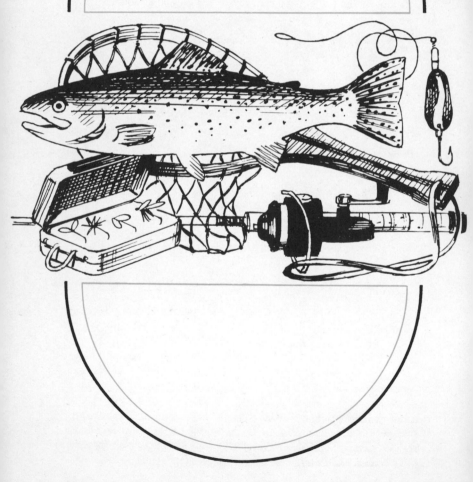

Sweet-water angling is undoubtedly one of the most popular forms of outdoor sport. Those who progress beyond the quick-dunk summer-camp style of fishing quickly learn that there is a lot more than luck involved in making consistent catches. They learn of the sophisticated techniques that have developed around each phase of the sport. They discover a rich field of literature that traces angling from the early recorded history of man. The fanatics among us sometimes give up other pursuits almost entirely to devote every spare moment to the game—even going so far as to become addicted to following one type of fish. But the most fortunate anglers are those young-at-hearts who are content to fish anywhere for anything any time they can get out.

■ When fishing for largemouth or smallmouth bass, regardless of your choice of tackle, never forget that you are fishing for two species with different habits. Look for smallmouth in rocky environments—over drop-offs, around rocky rubble shores, off stone points. Sometimes, especially on calm evenings, they can be taken off weed beds near shore. Smallmouth bass *generally* respond to smaller baits than largemouths. During spring breeding season, though, they'll knock big surface plugs right out of the water. Largemouths more frequently respond to big baits but will attack the tiniest crappie jig if it's Yo-Yo'd past a nest.

Spinners, plain or trimmed with small pieces of pork rind, small fly-rod bugs, minnows, crickets, worms, crayfish, hellgrammites, shrimp, are all good baits for smallmouths. Yet these fish are finicky. What works one day may be flatly refused the next.

Largemouth bass locate their headquarters around underwater trees, stumps and brush piles. They slink along under lily pads like snakes. Bushy undercut banks are favored hiding holes. Though you can usually score on them in the shallows early and late, the big fellows move into deeper water when the sun climbs and the water warms. Use deep-water plugs or weighted baits for them then. They'll hit almost any large plug from huge plastic worms to prickly fly-rod poppers.

■ Both largemouth and smallmouth bass often want their artificial baits in the top twelve inches of water. At these times they'll refuse the most provocatively worked surface plug and the wriggliest underwater lure if it is too deep. In these cases, use an underwater lure, but in retrieving, hold your rod high over your head and crank fast. This keeps the sinking lure riding just under the surface.

■ Bass fishing is generally not very productive during extremely high or low atmospheric pressure periods. A *slow*-falling barometer also indicates poor fishing more often than not. Bass will bite better when the barometer is on a slow rise, but the very best conditions are during a fast fall.

■ Over the years, the color combination of red and white has maintained its popularity for largemouth bass plugs. The reason is simple. The combination offers a good contrast against most backgrounds and is effective when a dark sky makes surface water light or dim. Yellow is next in popularity because it keeps its color distinction for a long distance. White follows closely behind. The metallic or flash finishes, however, are presently most popular over a wide area of the country because they reflect the light when they move, making the distance from which they are visible greater than that of any standard color.

■ Even when the summer heat makes angling slow in impoundments, streams will usually provide good bass fishing. Because streams have a good water flow, their temperature is cool and their oxygen content high, which are favorable conditions for fish. Cold-water streams produce particularly scrappy smallmouths. When you are fly-fishing for them, use chunky-body flies and various sizes of streamers; for an ultralight spin rig, use small wobblers and spinners.

After spawning is over, bass often tend to school in the streams. Look for swirls in the water that sometimes give schooling bass away.

Some of the best largemouth stream fishing is to be had in the headwaters of brackish tidal creeks.

For all stream bass fishing, practice up on your accuracy casting. You'll need it to be able to place lures in the small pockets beneath overhanging branches.

■ Here's the most effective way to rig a plastic worm for bass. Clip the nose from the worm so that the end is perfectly flat. Cut a bell-type sinker in half; remove the wire swivel if there is one. A bullet-shaped sinker remains. Thread the line through the sinker, and attach it to a number 2 or number 4 hook. Bend the hook shank back slightly so that the barb is offset from the eye. Feed the barb into the head of the worm so that it comes out on the bottom about a quarter of an inch back. Pull the barb out, twist it and the bend around so that the barb is facing up and insert the barb back into the worm. The hook eye should be buried in the worm near the head. The sinker will rest on the line in front of the worm's nose. Stick a wooden toothpick or piece of wire through the worm and through the hook eye until it emerges from the other side. Clip the toothpick flush with the worm or wind the wire around the worm head, burying the ends again or simply bending them into the plastic. This rig can be worked at any depth since the plastic worm will float and can be controlled with the sinker.

■ You can use plastic worms on a fly rod if you doctor them slightly. Cut off the flat tail end. Cut off the head to a point just in front of the collar. Cut a strip out of the belly from the rear of the collar to the end of the worm. Rig up with a hook and toothpick as discussed above. Utilize a fast-sinking, sinking-tip or sinking-head line. In effect, you have streamlined the worm to fly-rod casting size.

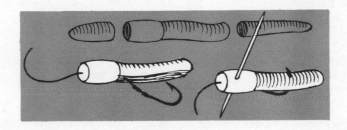

■ A floating plastic worm that isn't weighted can be snaked in and out of the brush or lily pads. The buried hook will keep it almost entirely weedless. But you must strike hard in order for the hook to penetrate both the plastic and the mouth of the fish.

■ In winter, the water depth bass favor is fifteen to thirty feet. Before ice-over, fish just off the bottom with live bait, with nonliving natural bait or with jigs. If you want, troll with a deep-diving lure or one with a planing device.

■ A tremendously effective combo lure for largemouths and smallmouths (you gear the size of the lure to the size of the fish) is a plug with a lead-head jig trailed about three feet behind it. Remove the rear treble hook from the plug. Hook a snap and swivel into the rear screw eye where the hook was. Tie three feet of mono to the swivel. Attach the jig directly to the mono. In early season, use a shallow-running or surface plug and the lightest jig you can find or make. Later, the size of the jig must be increased and the type of plug changed to a diver or even a lead-head, deep-sinking type.

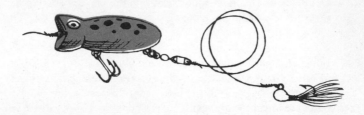

■ Jigger poling is an exciting method of clobbering bigmouths. It is widely used in the South, but there is no reason why it should not be more generally accepted than it is wherever largemouths and fishermen gather. You start with a strong but light cane pole with a limber end. Paint half the pole—from the tip down—dull green or duckboat brown. The pole should be picked in a twenty-foot length, but it is cut back (from the tip) to about eighteen feet. Tie in heavy mono (twenty- to thirty-pound test) to the middle of the pole. Wind it in big spirals to about four-and-a-half inches from the tip. At this point, make four or five turns around the bamboo and run the line through the turn loops drawing it down snugly. Tie a snap swivel to the end of the line approximately six inches from the tie on the pole so that just six inches of line will extend from the pole. Attach a jointed, solid or solid-with-spinners plug to the snap. The technique is as follows: Hold the butt in one hand and use the other hand to grasp the pole a few feet farther up. If you are moving along the

shore in a boat, jig the rod tip up and down, in and out of the water ahead of the plug, to create a bubbly wake and sound disturbance. In back swamp waters, the jigger poler runs his lure in figure eights, all the while slapping the water with the pole tip. This is the reason that the line is tied back from the tip four-and-a-half inches. It really works. And if you tie into a lunker with no whippy rod to absorb the shock, you'll find yourself in for a pleasant jolt.

■ For years, the fly-and-spinner combination has been used successfully on panfish and smallmouth bass. You can improve the design, however, by rearranging the traditional spinner-first-fly-after arrangement on most manufactured lures. Take a double willow-leaf spinner shank, cut off the forward blade and tie in a fly directly to the four-inch shaft. Flies that work include royal coachman, black gnat, McGinty and other attractor patterns. Snap in your hook, and you're all set. The motion of the lure seems to simulate that of a small minnow after a bug of some sort, and in the rocky shallows, smallmouths will clobber either.

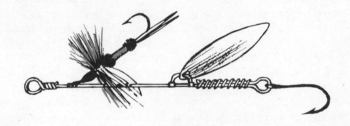

■ Here's how to get the most from early-season trout fishing—both in relaxing sport and hooked fish. Head for small brooks, streams, lakes and ponds. Fish in protected coves, near shore and where the current is slow. The surface waters of lakes and ponds are usually warmer than medium-sized trout streams early in the season. The small brooks do not have any giant currents for fish to battle. Also, at the season's start, most anglers will be elbow-to-elbow on the favorite larger bodies of water. If you must fish the bigger streams and rivers, stick to areas where the waters have overflowed their banks, slow-current pools and sloughs. Skip the heavy water.

■ When fishing small trout brooks, avoid the pretty, easy-access spots and dangle your bait or lure in the tough-to-reach places. Stick your rod through brush and branches just for one little dangle in a small pocket or hole. Fish hide in places like this, and most other anglers will pass such spots by because of the difficulty in working them.

■ During hot summer days, the standard advice has been to fish deep—in the thermocline—in lakes. Although this is good advice, do not ignore the inshore waters entirely. Early in the morning, rainbows and browns both make forays close to shore for baitfish before retreating to the depths for the rest of the day. Evening finds these trout moving in again for a quick sniff around, and the wise angler moves accordingly.

■ During fall, the major mayfly hatches are past. Trout then gorge themselves on terrestrial insects—ladybugs, grasshoppers and the like. Techniques are different, too. The usual upstream cast with drag-free drift can be altered as follows: Cast across or quartering downstream from time to time. Skitter flies on the surface, make bugs swim gently, twitch artificial grasshoppers. Trout get used to leaves and other debris drifting over them during autumn, and they snap at most things that give any indication of being alive. Use light terminal tackle, however. Low, clear water makes this a necessity.

■ Early in the season, an effective rig for trolling up trout in big waters is a fairly large spoon with the treble hooks removed from it. In place of the trebles, tie in a short length of monofilament with two single hooks tied in tandem. Thread a nightcrawler onto the

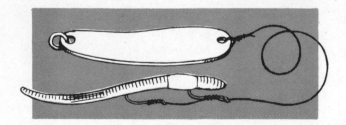

tandem. Begin trolling close to shore and' work slowly out. Use copper- or bronze-finished spoons on bright days, silver or nickel on cloudy days. Switch to other ploys a little later in the season when trout are quite awake and active and sure to spook from this monster rig.

■ Anglers using roe from big lake-run rainbows and browns often float it in nylon bags—made from women's discarded stockings—attached to the hook. Since repeated dunkings will cause the bait to lose natural color, you can substitute red or hot orange nylon net for the stocking material. The wider mesh will also make the offering look more natural.

■ Winter steelhead fishermen, who also utilize salmon or steelhead roe, have developed a method for using the bait without a bag. The skein of roe is dunked in powdered (not crystallized) borax to make it easier to handle as well as to preserve it. Small chunks are then cut from the skein in alternating diagonals from both sides—tail to head. Placed in a sealed container in the refrigerator, the chunks can be stored for two weeks; in the freezer, they will keep longer. When baiting up, pass your leader through the turned-up eye and tie it to the hook shank. You then have a loop along the shank which can fit over the roe gob. The pressure of a fairly tight line will keep it in place. About eighteen inches up the leader, tie in a double or three-way swivel with a nub of surgical tubing affixed to it. The tubing holds a section of "pencil" lead sinker which pulls free in case of hang-up.

■ Rather than clamping split shot directly to your leader, leave a four-inch whisker section when tying in the tippet. Attach the weight directly to that. It will cast easier, and you can usually remove the weight by simply sliding it down the dropper. This eliminates the need for clipping off the fly. You also do not risk nicking the leader with crimped-on shot. If the dropper breaks when you are fighting a fish, who cares?

■ When stream-wading, notice the position of the sun. Avoid having your back to it. Long shadows cast ahead of you on the water will spook fish for some distance.

■ Try hanging a strip of flypaper on a tree branch near the stream you plan to fish. Leave it there all afternoon. Check it and match your artificial flies to those caught in the trap.

■ Anglers who do much fishing in heavy brush-banked streams often make up a short rod especially for this situation. They install bigger guides and tip top than normal. This allows you to reel in both line and leader—with clip-on weights still attached—right through the guides up to the tip top where the hook catches. This way you do not have a length of line—from sinkers down to the hook—swinging about to wrap in the bushes. To change or replace bait, pull the rod back far enough to reach the hook, rest the butt on the ground, replace your bait and move the rod back through the brush. Release the line so that the terminal tackle will swing free, and you're in business again.

■ Great Lakes trout and coho anglers who fish from shore have devised a way to get more distance in their casts when using heavy fifteen- to twenty-pound-test line. The method can be used successfully by other fishermen who do not wish to clutter their lines with sinkers. The technique is to melt solder or lead into the inside upper half of a spoon to give additional weight. This weight does not seem to hinder lure action, and it increases casting distance immensely.

■ Where legal, two- and three-fly rigs are still effective in taking trout when single-fly offerings fail. Different patterns are used, tied three feet apart. The end fly is a wet nymph. The middle fly is a wet or dry, and the "hand" fly—the one closest to you—is a dry. The retrieve is most important. You pull in quick spurts with short pauses between. The hand fly occasionally skips over the water surface, the middle fly alternately skims and jumps, the tail fly is drawn through the water. Try flies of different sizes and patterns.

■ If the wind is blowing your dry flies out of compartmented plastic boxes, try putting small strips of magnetic tape into the bottom of each container section to hold the hooks without mashing or breaking hackles.

■ Silica gel crystals, crushed and placed in a small plastic bottle, are good substitutes for commercially made fly-dry. Just drop a soaked fly into the bottle, swirl it around a bit and it will be ready for use.

■ Metal lines for deep fishing are tricky to use. Lead-core line is more flexible than Monel and easier to use, but it doesn't sink as fast and deep when trolled. It packs best on big level-wind reels. It gets its strength from a woven nylon sheath, which should be frequently checked for frayed areas. Use a strong backing with a weaker leader when trolling with it. Solid wire line gets deeper but is harder to use. It must be played off a reel slowly to avoid coils springing out. Be extremely careful not to get kinks in it. If kinks develop, snip the line apart and splice it together again. Pumping a rod with wire line held in one spot will eventually cause metal fatigue at the point where the line bends over the tip top. To help avoid this problem, use a roller tip top and take line in and let it out slowly while trolling.

■ During the bright, hot midday periods on lakes or streams, try using a big, fluffy spider with long (two-inch) hackles. This will work, however, only in still pools. Raise the rod tip and pull back on the line simultaneously, causing the fly to literally skate across the surface. Long rods are in order, as are heavier tippets, to avoid twist and break-off when a fish roars up to clobber the fly.

■ When trolling in the spring for landlocked salmon, don't be afraid to use some speed. Zigzag a course along the shoreline toward which the wind is blowing. An erratic course will sink the lure to various depths and cover more territory. Also try rocky points and mouths of streams. You can try several passes in front of these areas.

■ When using oar power to troll for salmon, try digging hard, then coming almost to a dead stop. Repeat this to keep the lure dancing attractively.

■ Try using a wire spreader when trolling two flies for salmon. Good ones can be made from wire guitar, mandolin or banjo strings. Bend the string into two arms, one about seven inches long, the other five inches. Twist a loop into both arm ends and at the bend. Attach a barrel swivel before twisting the loop into the bend. Flies, of course, are attached to each arm end with monofilament. The resulting wire "wish bone" will open and close as it is trolled, causing the flies to wiggle most enticingly.

■ Long salmon leaders are advisable when you are trolling flies in calm water. You should use twenty-five or thirty feet of mono between the line and fly.

■ To troll steadily at the depth from which you hooked your first fish of the day, tie a line holding a two-ounce sinker to the stern of your boat. The sinker should hold six to eight inches underwater. Observe carefully the angle of the line holding the sinker when you get the first strike. Keep the sinker at exactly the same angle later; you'll be trolling the lure right where you want it.

■ A string of flashers (sometimes known as a troll) used after ice-out is a good attractor for salmon. Keep one of your lines, with a lure on it, up short ten to fifteen feet behind the flashers. Some of these trolls permit attachment of a lure directly behind on the same wire. This is a good rig for lakers, big browns and rainbows, too.

■ A good bait for catfish can be created from a hunk of well-aged Limburger cheese. Mix the cheese with a little flour. Then work a cotton ball into the flour-cheese mixture. Hook this wad and, if you can stand the smell, you're nearly certain to score.

■ Another fragrant catfish bait can be made with sponges. Cut a sponge into small cubes and put them in a jar. Add meat scraps and fish scraps, including entrails. Let the concoction ripen for a week. The oils will seep into the sponge pieces, giving them an odor that appeals greatly to catfish. If the above recipes are too aromatic, there are ready-made baits available whose odors are more endurable to you yet still attractive to the catfish.

■ Catfish like live bait as well as, if not better than, the stink baits usually presented by fishermen. Some of the best live offerings include crayfish, minnows and, the best of all, a big juicy night crawler.

■ Chum to hold panfish in one area. You can do this by putting meat or fish scraps in a mesh bag of the type onions come in and lowering it with weight. You can retrieve it to add more chum. Another way is to puncture a can of fish-based catfood all around the sides. Thread a line through two punched holes at the top. Lower the can to rest on the bottom, where it will give off a delightful aroma—to fish. Occasionally jerk the can or onion bag to keep things working.

■ Spring is the time for seeking walleyes in the daylight hours. They move into the shallows then, to spawn. You need to scratch the bottom for these fish. Use a bell sinker on a three-way swivel ahead of a june bug spinner with a single hook and live worm trailing it. Keep the sinker bouncing on the bottom as you troll slowly ahead. You can use a minnow instead of the worm behind the spinner, but a worm is best.

■ After the spring spawning period, walleyes head back to deep water. They're really creatures that prefer the dark, which is ample reason to fish for them after the sun sinks. During night hours, they move up from their deep holes. Try them deeper, too, at night, but chances are that you'll be able to hook them near the top.

■ Used flashbulbs can be painted with nail polish and used as extra bobbers. Wind a rubber band several times around the base of each bulb. When you want to put one on, just thread the line through the windings. The bobber will stay on securely and can be slid up or down the line to put a bait at any desired depth.

■ Trolling for panfish can often be more effective if you put your motor into reverse or, if you have no reverse, turn it one hundred eighty degrees so that the motor will pull the boat stern first. This will enable you to move ahead more slowly and to control the boat more easily at that speed. It will also prevent lines from entangling in the prop—particularly that of the motor operator if he is trolling too.

■ Drifting is another successful method for locating schools of panfish. If you have no motor and want to drift but the wind is too strong, make a sea anchor. Tie a metal bucket or, better, a canvas bucket to a strong line attached to your boat, and toss the whole works overboard. You can also make such an anchor from a piece of nylon cloth. It's then called a parachute anchor.

■ Add a little sardine or cod-liver oil to panfish flies. It will make them much more desirable.

■ Cleaning spiny panfish can cut up your hands painfully. Wear a pair of lightweight canvas or cotton gloves when doing this job, and sprinkle plenty of salt in the palms to help you grip the slippery fish.

■ Crappies and bluegills will both take worms, but in the hardware department, use flies and floating bugs for the bluegills and streamers, jigs or spinners for crappies.

■ Foam bugs—spiders, nymphs and the like—make top bluegill lures when rigged as follows. Put a single BB shot about eight inches ahead of the lure. Tie in a thin pencil float about six inches ahead of the split shot. The foam bug floats off the bottom but beneath the surface and follows the twitching retrieve. The little float indicates even the lightest hit. To eliminate the shot, wind enough fine lead wire (about an inch) just behind the hook eye of the foam bug to take it down slowly. Green spiders are a good choice in insect imitations.

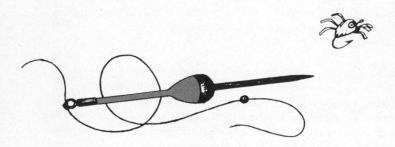

■ When fishing with bait for panfish, try using a floating bass plug as a bobber. It reacts very sensitively to any nibbles from the small fish—and you just might tie into a stray largemouth if you are working your bait with occasional twitches.

■ After bluegills leave the shallows and hole up in deeper water, try this rig while drifting or slow-trolling. Use a hook baited with worms or a fly tipped with a tiny bit of worm. Ten inches above the hook fix a medium-sized bobber. Then, about fifteen inches above the float, attach enough sinker to sink the rig. Work a pattern away from shore until you locate fish. The float will keep the hook just above the bottom on which the sinker drags.

■ Tiny pipe-cleaner-bodied bucktail jigs are as popular as minnows for taking crappies. But crappies are strange fish, and often you must present lures to them in a different manner from day to day. At times you just cast a jig and let it sink. The fish nab it on the way down. Other times you have to work the jig in short, snappy jerks. Some days they want it fast; on others you must retrieve slowly and easily.

■ When trolling for pike or pickerel, try holding the line in your hand as you paddle or row a boat. You get some terrific built-in action this way. Just be ready to drop the line so that you won't pop it.

■ When grasping a large pike by hand to release it, take your hold across the head with thumb and forefinger in the eye sockets (not in the eyes). The other fingers press firmly against the skull bone. Besides the teeth, be careful of the bones to the rear of a pike's head. They're sharp, too.

■ Pickerel and pike often go for a skittering bait—a frog or a strip of pork rind or fish belly will do well—worked across the weed beds. Use a long fly rod or cane pole for best effect, and keep the bait skating around steadily.

■ Large shiners, herring and suckers make good baitfish for pike. Alive they can be hooked in any of the numerous accepted ways, including the tandem-hook method. Two hooks in line—one large, one small—are utilized. The large hook is fastened with a rubber band to the side or belly of the baitfish aft of the dorsal fin. The small hook pierces the minnow's lips, anchoring him to the rig. The bait will last with good strength for a long while with this method.

■ The old saw about needing extra-big bait or lures for granddaddy pike is not necessarily true. Pike also go for three-eighths-ounce- to five-eighths-ounce lures—spoons or plugs—like thieves to an open safe.

■ When possible, fish for muskies just before rain (not an electrical storm) and during a light rain. Muskellunge are nearly always active during such periods.

101

■ Prime times for pike fishing are from 1:00 A.M. to 11:00 A.M. and from 3:00 P.M. to 4:00 P.M., based on the times that record fish have been taken over many years.

■ Cork or plastic foam strips glued to your fishing boat's gunwale make handy places to hook-hang lures until they dry. If you put wet lures back into a sealed tackle box, you're asking for rusted hooks.

■ To mark your monofilament lines for depth-finding and keeping track of the amount of line you had out when the last big fish hit, use a felt-tipped pen. Your partner can make a quick dabbing mark even as you are pulling your line out. The stuff dries fast and is easily wiped off.

■ A tiny split shot attached to one of the treble hooks of a spinning lure can impart a darting action to the lure as well as minimize line twist. This works better on some spinners (and wobblers) than others.

■ To keep grasshoppers alive longer on the hook, try this. Use a long-shank hook. Solder or glue two short pieces of thin, soft wire across it. Bend the wire bands around the hopper to attach him to the hook without impaling him. He'll kick up for a good long time this way.

■ Mix a few ounces of red brick dust into your worm bedding. The wigglers will, in a few days, develop a harmless rich red color that will make them more attractive to fish.

■ Dying minnows can be revived, for at least a little while, by dropping two or three aspirin tablets into the bait bucket.

Ice Fishing

To the uninitiated, ice fishing would seem to capture first prize for the foremost self-punishment award in outdoor pursuits. But there is something about trekking out on a wide expanse of slick glare ice to angle for fish through a floor of solid water that fishermen find fascinating. On bright days ice fishing can become a festive family sport that combines hiking, ice skating, eating huge meals and having fun in the fresh air. And with modern cold-weather clothing there is no reason for becoming chilled.

■ Deciding where in the ice to cut your fishing holes is not too difficult when you keep one factor in mind. The amount of dissolved oxygen in the water is the element most important in determining the presence of fish and the degree of their activity. Shallow lakes often run low in oxygen content during the latter part of the season. Snow-covered ice prevents plants from turning sunlight energy into oxygen. When such conditions prevail, cut fishing holes near known weed beds, spring holes (check a survey map of the lake bottom) or areas where the wind has blown the ice free of snow.

■ You can also use an electronic fish-finder to check out the bottom—right through the ice. Simply place a few drops of antifreeze and water on clear ice from which you have scraped away the snow. Place the transducer on this wet spot to get a clean reading. Different bottoms will give different readings, and you'll soon learn to distinguish from them where the weeds are, as well as how deep the water is, without having to cut a hole.

You can also scan for fish with the little sonar units. Cut a hole, lower the transducer (cocked at a slight angle) on a stick and slowly turn the instrument about. Gain should be set fairly low so that you don't pick up bottom yards away.

■ When using the electronic instruments for ice fishing, bring two sets of batteries. The spare can stay warmly wrapped in the car. When the signals begin to weaken, replace the battery with the one that has been protected.

Most newcomers to ice fishing don't rush right out to purchase an ice auger. They're expensive. Instead they use one of the traditional implements—an axe or an ice spud, which is a long-handled chisel affair—for cutting holes in the ice. Before using one of these tools, though, you should attach one end of a leather thong to the handle and the other end to your wrist. Without this safety strap, choppers will frequently slip from your grip during the final stroke and descend into the frigid depths.

■ It pays to mark fishing holes that have been top producers. Very likely a spot where you catch fish one day will provide fairly good action the next. Jam a small branch or stick into the hole just before you leave for the day. The hole will be starting to ice over at that time, and in a few minutes the marker will be frozen fast. Knot on a bit of colored rag or plastic so that you will be able to locate it quickly on the next trip.

■ If you chop your fishing hole, make sure its edges are cut smooth to avoid the possibility of fraying line. Inevitably, a large fish will run the line out horizontally. All it takes is a little seesawing against sharp ice to pop the line and lose the lunker.

■ Instead of buying a special short jigging rod, try using the tip of your standard spinning or fly rod (not a good bamboo rod, naturally). "Pack rods" that take down into at least four sections provide even shorter wands for jigging.

■ Ice fishermen often take a trick from the bag of their warm-weather brethren to keep live minnows healthy. In summer, minnow dunkers have found that their bait stays cool longer when stored in an inexpensive plastic-foam ice chest. You can use the same method in winter to keep baitfish from freezing. Instead of placing the container holding them directly on the ice, set it inside the foam cooler.

■ If you use a large bobber or heavy sinker, fish will quickly detect the unnatural resistance these items cause—especially during winter when fish tend to take the bait more slowly and cautiously. Also, remember to wait until your light bobber is well underwater before striking.

■ Bluegills and other sunfish tend to school in slightly deeper water during winter than in summer. Look for them in depths of twelve to twenty feet—but just off weed beds.

■ It's often wise to cut several ice holes close together when you experience a sudden flurry of action. You'll most likely take a good helping of fish during a short period of time before a roving school heads for safer waters.

■ Arrange your tip-ups in a pattern around a point of land, following the shore curve within coves or other likely areas, but save one to set out some distance from the others. It's not uncommon for the lone picket to produce. If it does, try moving the other baits out slightly.

■ If the kids aren't using their sleds, you can make good use of them for hauling tackle, food, stove and shelter out on the ice. Runner sleds are fine when the snow isn't piled up too deeply. Or you can make a sled specifically designed for ice fishing from broken skis or toboggan runners, possibly picked up free at sporting-goods shops or winter resort areas that have rental services. Mount a good-sized wood box on your creation in which to carry your equipment.

■ Scraping a lead sinker with a knife blade will expose shiny new metal that will act as an additional attractor to your bait.

■ Ice holes are often chummed with the following enticements: rice, corn, oatmeal, peas, beans, cracker or bread crumbs, even egg shells. The latter are from hard-boiled eggs. Simply save the shells from peeled eggs, crumble them in your hands and sprinkle them into the hole. The little pieces, which twist and flash whitely going down, are effective in stimulating lethargic fish metabolism. Do not overdo the chumming. Sprinkle a pinch or three of whatever you are using. Pause a few minutes before repeating. If fish start coming in, chum almost continually, but sparingly, to hold them.

■ When fishing relatively shallow for panfish species, stay with a hole fifteen or twenty minutes before shifting to a new one. If you're after such deeper-water species as lake trout, walleyes and perch, stick with a hole an hour or more before changing.

■ When jigging through the ice, go to water as deep as sixty feet for perch (which succumb easily to this method). When fishing with lures, use a gentle pulsating action—the "thrumming" rods are good for this. When jigging with bait, vibrate your offering by using wrist action alone for a few seconds; then, suddenly, raise your entire rod arm to shoulder height. Follow this by slowly sinking the bait again. Keep up the rhythm.

■ To keep steel leaders from curling when you are coiling up line, staple a large rubber band to the end of the tip-up opposite the spool. Leave the leader unwound when coiling up the line. Lock the spool by closing the tip-up; place the hook beneath the rubber band. The resultant tension will keep the metal leader from kinking.

■ Hook live minnows on one side of the dorsal, instead of right under the fin, through to the other side in the usual manner. This method keeps the baitfish stronger longer.

■ A piece of heavy-duty aluminum foil covering a hole will help keep your line from freezing to the cut ice edges. Line frozen in this manner can set up a resistance that will cause a fish to drop your bait like a hot coal. Simply make a slit in the foil, run the line through and weight the foil to the ice to prevent its being blown away by the wind.

■ When snow covers the ice, scrape it away for a distance of four or five feet around each hole. The light filtering through the ice will often attract fish.

■ Vegetable-dyed nonliving natural baits are often more attractive to fish than baits in the original color. Favored hues are purple, blue and yellow.

■ Because bobbers painted black absorb more heat from the sun, they won't ice up as quickly as those painted other colors.

■ If you don't have a standard steel or file for sharpening your auger, wrap fine sandpaper or emery cloth around a magazine or newspaper that has been rolled into a cylinder. Use this device to hone the inside, or cupped, edges of the auger's blades.

■ A handy warming stove can be fashioned from a pail or large coffee can. Cut holes around the sides near the bottom; if you choose to cover the heater with a pie tin or foil, cut some at the top, too, for ventilation. The fuel is charcoal. If you wish, you can put a smaller water-filled tin can atop the coals. Occasionally pour the warmed water into your fishing holes to prevent ice-over.

Fishing Tackle Care

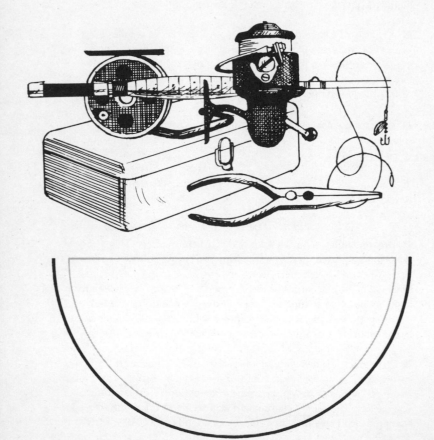

Even the toughest fishing equipment requires a certain amount of care. Most tackle overhauls, understandably, are scheduled for winter, but some maintenance procedures, such as oiling, cleaning and making minor repairs, should be carried out between trips all through the season.

■ To unstick a jointed rod when the standard front-of-the-chest or hip-side steady pull (never twist) fails, put the rod behind your back. Place your hands on either side of the ferrules, palms down, wide enough spread so that they are snug against your buttocks at the sides. Your arms are straight back along your sides. Keeping the grip tight, slowly bend your knees and begin to take a sitting posture. Your hips will force your hands apart at the wrists, thus pulling apart the rod.

■ The reason that rods jam in the first place is because they are dirty or corroded. An old method of keeping metal ferrules lubricated is to run the male end through your hair or alongside your nose to pick up oil. Used sparingly, this method will do. Too much oil, though, can cause the ferrules to pick up grit or the rod sections to slip out of alignment. Well-fitting metal ferrules really should not have to be oiled if they are kept perfectly clean. Use lighter fluid and a cotton swab. Rub the ferrules with silver polish if they are pitted. You can use a rifle-bore brush to clean the female ferrule. Glass ferrules on the newer rods require only an occasional touch of lip pomade to keep them fitting snugly.

■ Fishing creels can become rather messy during a season of heavy use. Try cleaning yours with a solution of a half cup household ammonia added to a quart of water. Then hang the creel in the fresh air for a day.

■ If you don't have a leader book or packet, store your ready leaders in coils, using a snip of pipe cleaner to hold each coil together. This way there's no risk of tangling.

■ Insect repellent can play havoc with the finish on fly lines (as well as that of many other plastic articles). Don't forget to rinse your hands thoroughly after applying bug juice, no matter how fantastically the fish are rising.

■ Strips of reflector tape placed on net handles, tackle boxes and gaffs will help you locate these items more easily at night.

■ Modern fly lines can be stored on reels through the winter without taking on a permanent set. However, today's lines may develop some kinks, especially if you have a small reel. These are easily removed by simply hand-stretching the line, then laying it in loose coils off the reel for half a day.

■ At least once during a season of heavy fishing, your reels should be taken completely apart and cleaned. Use water or possibly a mild soapy solution on all surfaces. Wash the parts—except those of nylon—in lighter fluid. Then dab graphite lubricant sparingly onto the gears. A touch of oil—especially for level-wind reels—in oil holes, a check for worn parts, and you're ready to reassemble.

■ Desiccants which lubricate and actually absorb water residue are recommended for use on all kinds of fishing equipment and firearms. But some of this stuff leaves a residual odor which, if it taints your line, could result in fewer bites. When you apply it, be careful not to apply too much or get it on the line.

■ A woman's discarded nylon stocking makes a sensitive detector for finding rough spots in rod guides. Simply run the stocking through the guide slowly, feeling for hangups, listening for the clicking sound as nylon fibers snap on rough spots. Emery cloth is good for smoothing these spots out, but if there is a visible groove in the hand guide (closest to the reel) and in the tip top, it's time to replace them.

■ Sometimes monofilament fishing line has been stored in tackle shops for too long. Check its appearance by looking for a white powdery patina that indicates age and decomposition. Fortunately, many manufacturers are now sealing their products in vacuum packages to prevent this.

■ When you are casting, the front end of braided or mono line takes the brunt of abuse. It is wise to cut off from four to six feet of line after every couple of fishing trips. When a strong fish drags line into the rough or, in saltwater party-boat fishing, into the hooks and lines of other fishermen or over rocks or along the side of the boat, great damage can be done. Sharp teeth of some fish can also do dirty work. Carefully examine as much line as you had out, either while you're fishing—the easiest way—or before the next trip. Frayed, peeled or nicked line must be cut off even if it means a great deal of waste. It isn't worth losing a good fish (plus the line and tackle from the damaged spot on) because of false economy.

■ Because small boats are not equipped with rod holders, many good rods and reels are ruined in them. The traditional way to stow rigged tackle when running is simply to lay the gear down the quickest way. Heavy feet, weather, entanglements, sudden moving of equipment—all can damage equipment jammed between seats or laid on the deck. Rod holders for small boats are now commercially produced, but you can make your own very simply. Hardware stores carry spring clips for keeping broom handles and similar items in place. Epoxy or screw the clips to a thwart, the side of a seat or along the gunwale so that the rods may be placed butt down, tip up, when the boat is running. Clip-type clothespins will work, too.

■ Instead of using plastic bottles—which can crack—try a large safety pin to hold swivels and snaps. Just thread the terminal tackle onto the pins using different pins for swivels and snaps of different sizes.

■ If your fly leader won't sink, try boiling it in water for a few minutes. Toothpaste rubbed on it works, too, as do the better commercial ointments especially created for the job.

■ Regular car wax (without cleaner) will protect fine bamboo rods from the elements—especially where salt water is a factor. You can also use it (sparingly) on the ferrules.

■ A rigged rod can be made safe for transporting in a car by wrapping heavy-duty aluminum foil around the hooks and sinkers. This will keep sinkers from bashing the finish or guide wrappings and will also keep hooks from snagging clothes—or you.

■ Consider keeping a small bottle of clear fingernail polish in your tackle box in case rod windings become frayed while you're on a trip.

■ Cleanerless car wax can be rubbed on the contact lip of your spinning reel spool for smoother, longer casts.

■ Pine or spruce pitch heated with a match or lighter can be used as emergency cement for rod guides or metal ferrules. Don't forget to get the real stuff, though, when you return home.

■ Use an empty egg carton in the following fashion when dismantling a reel for cleaning: Place each part type in a separate compartment, in order, as you go along. Reassembling, then, is made easy since you just pick up the parts in reverse order.

■ Melted catfish fat is an excellent preservative in which to soak your trotlines.

■ Cigarette filters make serviceable hook holders. You can stick small hooks along the sides and large hooks in the ends. Filters can also be used for popping bugs. A long-shank hook is stuck lengthwise into the filter. The hook eye protrudes from one end. It is then a simple matter to attach a leader. Small soft corks can be used too.

■ Torn plastic worms can be easily repaired by holding the ripped sections together over the fire of a cigarette lighter to fuse them. Give the plastic a chance to cool so that the joint will be fast and strong.

■ If you don't own a commercially made box for storing plastic worms, these great lures can be kept from melting by stowing them in a jar of water.

General Hunting Tips

The following ideas can be adapted to many kinds of hunting and will add to your fun, your chances of success, your comfort and your safety.

■ Most animals are partly or completely color blind. Wearing a bright color won't give your presence away. What they *do* detect visually is movement or a large block of solid color that looks unnatural in the surroundings. A plaid hunting jacket won't spook game even if it has red in it, as long as the plaid design breaks up the blocks of color effectively. At least one clothing manufacturer offers camouflage clothing that has a bright red background but is broken up by a conventional foliagelike pattern of dark splotches. Similarly, the blaze orange of safety-colored hunting garments will be no detriment in most types of hunting. Among the best of the blaze orange items is a cap or shoulder pull-on. It puts the color up high enough to be seen by anyone else in the woods, and if you're ever lost, it can be used to wave at a search plane.

■ Many hunters carry a length of string for pulling a patch through a gun bore to clean it. But in small-bored rifles, the string may "hang up" and refuse to drop all the way through. The solution is to attach a small fishing sinker or other soft weight (which won't mar the bore) to one end of the string. Just make sure before going afield that the sinker is small enough to drop through the bore easily.

■ In another section of this book, it is mentioned that mud, snow and other obstructions should be kept out of a gun bore; you should check the bore if you stumbled. When hunting in deep snow or muddy areas, cornfields or heavy brush, you should check it frequently.

■ Whether or not he realizes it, the average shotgun hunter never really uses his gun's front bead when making fast shots. What he actually does is swing and point the barrel itself, ignoring the bead. Nevertheless, having an easily visible bead is a help, especially in pass shooting or other hunting situations permitting a long, deliberate swing—just as it's helpful in trapshooting. If the bead on your gun doesn't show up well in poor light, you can replace it with one of a better color (brass instead of ivory, for instance, or the glowing orange-pink plastic kind). Or you can dab it with bright red nail polish.

■ In cold weather, your hands will stay warm longer if you don't have to remove your mittens to fumble around in your pocket for shells to reload your gun. Simply sew two or three cartridge loops onto the back of your left mitten (assuming that you are right-handed), insert the shells and pluck them out when necessary.

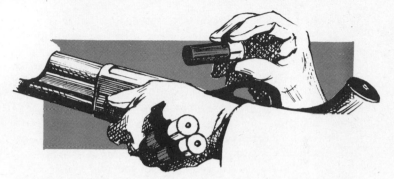

■ Make your stalk even more silent by pulling on an old pair of thick cotton or wool socks over your boots. Now you will be able to move almost soundlessly through dry, crackling leaves.

■ Regardless of what kind of game you have taken, the meat will be better if you dress and cool it as soon as possible, and be sure you have a copy of the *Wild Game Cookbook*, a popular title in the Remington Sportmen's Library.

■ For a scoped rifle, an optical collimator, available at gun shops, is useful for speeding up the job of zeroing and also for checking later to see whether it has retained its zero. The device is a very short tube that fits in above the muzzle and held in proper position by a small stud that fits into the barrel. (Good collimators have interchangeable studs for several calibers.) The tube contains a reticle with a grid printed on it. With the collimator in place, you adjust the scope so that the crosshairs are properly centered on the grid as you sight through the scope. Do *not* make the mistake of assuming that the rifle is now sighted in at, say, 100 yards. What you can assume is that your shots will now be on the paper and fairly close to the bull's-eye at about that distance so that with only a few more shots and additional minor scope adjustments, you will be perfectly sighted in. Afterward, you can reattach the collimator to see where the crosshairs show on the grid with the scope sighted in. Make a note of it, and pack the collimator along on a hunting trip so that you can quickly recheck whether the scope has shifted off its zero setting.

■ Not only distance but altitude, barometric pressure and the normal knocking about of a hunting trip can affect the bullet's point of impact with a scope that was previously sighted in. When you reach base camp, take a few minutes and a few shells to check your zero and trajectory at what you expect will be the most likely range.

■ If you are lacking a collimator, there's another way to speed up the zeroing job. Begin with a target at twenty-five yards. Shoot from a benchrest or solidly positioned table, with sandbag supports under your forward hand or the rifle's fore-end and under the heel of the buttstock. Align the crosshairs on the center of the bull's-eye and fire a shot—carefully. Check through the scope to see where the bullet struck, and then adjust the instrument to center the crosshairs on the bullet hole instead of on the bull's-eye. Now you know that the scope is set to sight approximately where the bullets are striking, though you've had to fire only one shot. Naturally, the point of impact will change at 100 yards, but not enough to put you off the target paper. With a target now set up at that range, it will take but a few more shots to finish sighting in.

■ If you're a handloader. remember that top accuracy is usually achieved with slightly *less* than maximum charges and that extra hot loads will not necessarily assure you of clean game hits. Follow the instructions and tables in a standard loading manual, working up slowly from mild loads to more potent loads. As you work up, check each new batch of loads for accuracy and pressure signs. The slightest cratering of primers usually indicates pressure—meaning that the load is too hot for perfect safety. Also bear in mind that brass wears out with repeated reloading and firing. After cleaning the empties, check each one. Any case with even the smallest flaw should be discarded.

■ Carry a pair of good-sized plastic food or refuse bags in your game pocket. They can be slipped over your boots to keep your feet dry if you have to cross a stream. They can be sat on to keep your bottom dry. They can be used to keep sandwiches or other foods dry, fresh and clean. And they can be used to hold small game or the heart and liver of big game that has been field-dressed so that you won't stain your game pocket.

■ When it's snowing, wrap a red kerchief around a rifle's scope and action to keep snow off the lenses and to help keep the action from freezing up. It's quicker to whip off a kerchief than to remove lens caps, and the red color has safety value in the woods.

Shooting Tips

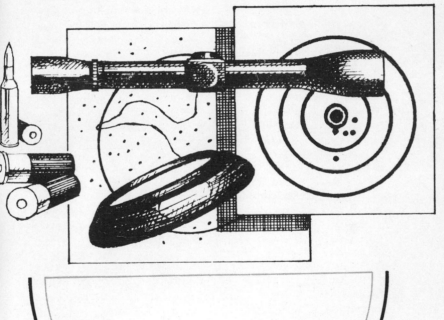

A gun is no more dangerous than any other item of outdoor recreational equipment when handled properly. That means following certain rules. Always treat every gun with the respect due a loaded gun. Always keep guns cased while going to or from a shooting area. When not actually hunting or target shooting, keep guns unloaded and either open the actions or disassemble takedown types. Always be sure that the barrel and action are clear of obstructions and that you have only the proper ammunition for the gun being used. Remove oil and grease from the chamber and bore before doing any firing. Carry a gun so that you can control muzzle direction even if you stumble, and keep the safety mechanism on until you're ready to shoot. If you are not absolutely sure of your target, don't pull the trigger. Never point a gun at anything you don't intend to shoot; even when dry-firing an empty gun, the target should be a legitimate one. Never engage in any horseplay while handling guns. Make sure unattended guns are unloaded. Store guns and ammunition separately, out of the reach of careless adults as well as children. Never climb a tree or fence or jump a ditch while holding a loaded gun. Never pull a gun toward you muzzle-first. Never shoot a bullet at a flat, hard surface or at the surface of water, as resulting ricochets and fragmentation can be dangerous. At target practice or during a plinking session, make sure your backstop is adequate. And finally, avoid alcoholic drinks before and during shooting.

■ Shooting glasses are a fine idea, regardless of whether you need prescription lenses. Their shatterproof feature is a good safety precaution, and the tinted kind will cut down the glare that sometimes interferes with aiming.

■ Ear protectors are strongly recommended for long shooting sessions—when you're practicing at a range, for example, or testing handloads or sighting in several rifles. The earmuff type is the most efficient when using arms that produce a really sharp crack. For guns with a less disconcerting report, the plug-in type will do.

■ The world's most popular rifle has long been the 22 rimfire. It's perfect not only for practicing, target shooting and many kinds of small-game hunting but also for learning purposes and for correcting mistakes made by even experienced marksmen. A rimfire rifle is relatively inexpensive and the ammunition even more so, which means that a tight budget needn't curtail practice. Its low noise level and virtual lack of recoil are equally important. The recoil of a big-bored, powerful rifle, sometimes combined with a very loud report, occasionally results in a shooter's habitually flinching every time he squeezes the trigger. The flinch pulls the rifle off target, ruining accuracy. The way to cure it is with lots of 22 practice. You might even start by dry-firing a 22 rifle until the flinch is under control; then do plenty of shooting with it before going back to a more powerful arm. The procedure recommended for beginners is to start with a 22, then graduate to something with only a little recoil, perhaps a 222, followed by something in the 6 mm. class, and so on. Following this gradual progression, a shooter will feel comfortable firing more and more powerful hunting arms.

■ Whether you're learning or just brushing up, try the prone shooting position first because it's so comfortable and steady. Stand facing the target squarely. Then turn about halfway to the right (if you're right-handed) and lie down at this angle to the target. Place your left elbow on the ground so that your arm is well up under the rifle, with the stock's fore-end lying flat in your palm. Spread your

legs out comfortably with your feet lying flat. Relax. The elbow of your shooting arm should also be on the ground and your shooting hand around the pistol grip, or wrist, of the stock so that the pad of your index finger—the area between the tip and the first joint—can easily rest on the trigger.

■ Whether you're shooting from the prone position or from some other position, the all-important sight picture remains the same. The front sight should be straight up and aligned in the center of the rear notch or aperture. The top of the front sight should be even with the top of the rear notch, or centered in an aperture. Visually, the two sights now blend together as if they were one. It takes only the slightest movement to change the point of aim, and you align this front-and-rear-sight blend so that the top of the front sight is just level with the bottom of the bull's-eye—as if the target were resting on the sight. This is called the six-o'clock hold. Once it's mastered, it can be varied on occasions when a shooter must hold over or hold under, depending on known bullet trajectory and estimated target distance, but it is the only correct basic sight picture.

■ Once in position and with the correct sight picture, take a deep breath and let out about two-thirds of it. Then hold the remainder but stay relaxed. Gently begin the trigger squeeze, taking up the slack until the slightest additional pressure will fire the rifle. (You can judge that pressure with a given trigger after firing the rifle a few times.) A slightly interrupted trigger squeeze is best because the sight picture will waver a little with your heartbeats and the final trigger "let-off" must come at the instant the wavering sights come exactly on target.

■ The sitting position is almost as steady as the prone, and in the field it can sometimes be made even more solid by sitting back *against* something—a tree, boulder, cliff, whatever. Face halfway to the right from the target as you sit on the ground, and draw your knees up comfortably. Keep your feet wide apart and the heels braced or dug in. Lean forward, bracing your left elbow over or just inside your left knee and your right elbow inside the right knee. You can then line the sights up very steadily.

■ The kneeling position is less steady than the others, but it is required in some competitions and there are hunting situations in which you can't see the game from the lower-to-the-ground prone or sitting positions. Kneel with your left knee up, pointed toward the target, and your right buttock on your right heel (or foot if your ankle is limber enough). Your left elbow is braced on or just in front of your left knee. Lean forward slightly for good balance, and you'll be reasonably steady.

■ The offhand, or standing, position feels the most natural but is the least steady of all. It, too, is required in competition as well as in some hunting situations. Stand with your left side toward the target, your feet parallel and about twelve inches apart. The fore-end again lies flat in your left palm, but pull your left elbow in directly under the stock. Your right elbow is lifted parallel with the gun and your upper arm is horizontal. Some shooters find that they can maintain a steadier hold by lifting the elbow of the shooting arm even higher. You may find that pulling your left hand in, nearer to your body, so that the elbow is braced against your waist, will help steady you. This forms a pedestal, and the bottom of the trigger guard can now rest on your left thumb while the fore-end rests on the tips of your fingers. This is a correct offhand target-shooting stance.

■ When hunting with a rifle, you should modify the standard positions by using a support, or rest, whenever possible. This simply means having something on which to rest your forward hand or arm. Don't rest the stock or barrel directly on any hard support, as the gun will bounce away slightly upon firing, throwing you off target. But with your hand or arm between the rifle and the support, you'll have the steadiest possible field hold. The rest can be a log, rock, tree trunk or stump—anything that presents itself. Even a rolled-up jacket or a pair of binoculars placed under your forward hand as you lie prone will increase your accuracy.

■ The basic sight picture of a handgun is the same as that of a rifle. However, since the sights of a handgun are farther from your eyes, you'll find that keeping both the sights and the target sharply in focus is nearly impossible. Most accomplished handgunners focus on the sights, letting the target go fuzzy. It may seem strange, but if you do this, you'll still see the target well enough to achieve good accuracy. If the sights are fuzzy, proper alignment will be impossible.

■ Except in formal target handgunning (for which both instruction books and a coach are strongly recommended), there is little sense in using anything but a two-handed hold. A handgun is extremely difficult to keep steady with one hand, and there's no reason to try when hunting. Rest the heel of your shooting hand in the cupped palm of your other hand and keep both arms as straight as possible. With the two-hand hold and both arms extended, you can use the same basic body positions as with a rifle. However, you will be facing the target squarely or nearly so. As with a rifle, your knees will brace your elbows or upper arms in the sitting position and one knee will brace one arm in the kneeling position.

■ On either a rifle or a handgun, the sight picture changes when a scope is used. The six-o'clock hold is now abandoned, and the crosshairs (or other reticle) must be centered not under but right against the middle of the target area.

■ If you tape the trajectory figures for a particular load to your rifle or its scope, you won't have to rely on memory in holding over or under for a target at a particular estimated range.

■ A few (very few) shooters do well with a shotgun by holding it in the same manner as a rifle. Even those who succeed are handicapping themselves. Whereas a rifle is held stiffly, to be aimed at a precise point and prevented from wavering, a shotgun must be held in a fluid manner to be able to be swung with a moving target. The forward hand cradles the fore-end, as far out as is comfortable. The thumb and fingers ride along the sides; don't wrap them up around the barrel. Don't try to keep your elbow directly under the gun, as you do with a rifle. Keep the elbow somewhat out to the side for smooth control of the swing. The shooting hand and arm are held differently, too. The elbow is lower, again for smooth swinging. The thumb wraps around over the pistol grip. On a single-trigger shotgun, the index finger curls over the trigger and pulls it instead of squeezing it. On a double-trigger model, the ball of the index finger is used, but only so that it can be slid quickly back to the rear trigger for a second shot.

■ You must get on a bird or other moving game quickly with a shotgun, mounting it to your shoulder, bringing the gun to your face to meet the rising comb with your cheek and swinging with the direction of the target all in one smooth sweep. It will help if, with the upper part of your body, you lean *slightly* forward, in the direction in which the gun is pointing. The upper body follows the barrel and target as you pivot from the waist.

■ Follow-through is vital in shotgunning. Swing the bead through the target and pull the trigger at the instant the lead seems right, but never let the gun stop at that instant or you'll be behind the target. Keep swinging as you pull the trigger, just as a golfer follows through with his swing after he has hit the ball.

■ Much has been written about the value of patterning a shotgun, but not all the comments have been accurate. The most important reason to pattern a shotgun is to find out whether the pellets are striking where they should be striking.

If a gun shoots considerably high or low or to the left or right, you should consult a gunsmith. With a single-barreled gun he can probably correct the fault at small expense. With a double, you may just have to remember where it patterns and do your own compensating as you shoot. Another reason to pattern a shotgun is to check whether you're using the right choke (and are therefore getting the desired density of pattern) for a particular kind of shooting. The least important reason is to check on the uniformity of pattern you're getting from your ammunition. With modern plastic shotgun shells uniformity can almost be taken for granted, and this also goes for handloads if they're carefully put together according to the tables in the loading manuals.

■ To pattern a shotgun, you can buy commercial patterning sheets or make your own simply by drawing a thirty-inch circle on a large sheet of paper. You fire at the center of this target from forty yards. Naturally, each pellet from a shotgun isn't going to strike in the same way on every shot; you're looking for the average kind of pattern you're getting. Most shooters therefore draw their conclusions from the patterns produced on at least five sheets, using the same load for each pattern. After firing one shell at each target, count the holes in each. (To do this easily, fold the target in quarters and count one quarter at a time, marking each hole with a pencil as you count.) To determine the density of pattern—the percentage of pellets in your load that strikes within the circle—divide the number of pellets contained in that load into the number you counted in the circle and multiply by 100. Then you add the percentages of all the targets and divide by the number of targets to get the average. An improved-cylinder choke gives you approximately 50 percent in a thirty-inch circle at forty yards; a modified choke should give you approximately 60 percent or so and a full choke should give you approximately 70 percent or better. A look at the pattern sheets will also tell you whether the shot is spread with reasonable uniformity and whether the heaviest concentration is pretty well centered in the circle.

■ The fit of a shotgun to the individual shooter is just as important as the fit of a rifle. If you don't feel comfortable—supple—with your gun or if you're not shooting as well as you think you should, ask your gunsmith about a fitting. Expensive custom-made guns are, of course, fitted to your specifications, but mass-produced arms must be made to fit the average shooter—and no individual is precisely average. Your gunsmith may be able to alter the stock slightly at reasonable cost and thus improve your shooting tremendously.

■ If you're shooting high, time after time, your shotgun's stock may be too long or the comb too high or you may not be keeping your head down against it. If you're shooting low, the trouble may be a too-short or too-low comb.

Small-Game Hunting

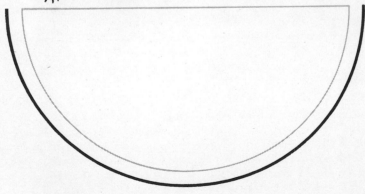

Until quite recently, the term *small game* was generally considered to include rabbits and squirrels and not much else. But many creatures—such as raccoons, woodchucks, prairie dogs, foxes, coyotes, bobcats and crows—although often labeled "varmints," have a role to play in nature, and when they're not overabundant, some of them actually beneficially fill a niche in the ecology.

■ If you are going to use a shotgun for squirrels, use one with a modified choke. The gauge can be 12, 20 or even 28, but the charges should be heavy—especially for hunting in tall timber. Express loads carrying No. 6 shot are recommended. Many hunters prefer a scatter gun because they feel that shooting at squirrels that are running furnishes the best sport. Others, however, prefer to still-hunt and stalk or to take a stand (often wearing camouflage clothing) and wait them out, shooting only at stationary targets and sometimes at a considerable range. These hunters generally use a scoped 22 rimfire rifle. If you want to test your marksmanship and at the same time save as much meat for eating as possible, you can restrict yourself to making head shots, using high-velocity 22 long rifle cartridges with either solid bullets or hollow-points. However, hollow-points should not usually be used for squirrel hunting because their expansion will ruin edible portions and because standard velocity is sufficient for ordinary woods hunting, though faster stuff is useful if you take most of your bushytails at relatively long range. In that case, you can also use a 22 rimfire magnum or, a 5mm. rimfire magnum.

■ Some squirrel hunters prefer to zero in a 22 rimfire rifle at 50 yards, figuring that the shortest shots might be as close as about 20 yards and the longest ones not much beyond 75 yards. With the rifle sighted at 50, there will be no need to hold much under or over at the other distances. However, most 22 shooters prefer a 100-yard zero, which requires holding just a little low at 50 and a little high at anything beyond 100. It is useful not only for squirrels but for rabbits, woodchucks at moderate range, crows, gophers, prairie dogs, etc.

■ For hunting squirrels, your scope power can be from 2 ½ X up to 4X, depending on the distance of most of your shots. Where handguns are legal for hunting, some marksmen prefer them for small game. Shots made with open sights should be at very short range. If you scope a handgun, the magnification can be from about 1.3X to 2X. Higher power isn't needed because few people can hold a pistol steady enough to hit a small target at more than thirty-five or forty yards. Greater magnification will also amplify the apparent wavering of the sight picture.

■ One of the two most popular methods of hunting squirrels is to walk as slowly and silently as possible through the woods, watching everything from the ground to the treetops for the twitch of a tail, a patch of gray—whatever shows—and listening carefully both for the scrabbling sound of running or climbing squirrels and for their chatter.

■ The other most popular method is to arrive before dawn at a likely spot and sit motionless at the base of a tree, boulder or stump that offers a good view of the surroundings. Squirrels are not nocturnal; you want to be present—and inconspicuous—when they emerge from their nests. They're good at staying out of sight when they see or hear anything alarming. But woods that seem barren when you move about noisily can come alive when you're still. If you have no luck in the early morning, be there and waiting motionless again before dusk; those are the times during which squirrels are most active.

■ When working through timber for squirrels, try to keep the sun at your back so that you'll have good shooting visibility at targets above ground level.

■ Some hunters learn to imitate the clicking, clucking, sometimes squeaking, chatter of squirrels. You can make some of the clicking and clucking sounds with your mouth and intersperse the squeakier clucks by sucking the back of your hand—a trick that sometimes lures foxes, too, if you don't have a predator call with you. (But for a fox, make the sounds smaller and squeakier, like those of a frightened mouse.) One of the best kinds of commercial calls is the type that uses an accordionlike rubber bellows to produce a chatter when you shake it. You can quickly become proficient with this mechanical gadget, which requires no oral skill. Lacking both a commercial call and oral skill, pick up a couple of rocks the size of tennis balls and click them together rapidly. If this improvised call is answered by squirrel chatter, repeat it briefly and then remain still, waiting for the approach of an inquisitive squirrel or two.

■ When prowling the woods for squirrels, check the ground for fallen acorns or other nuts that look freshly gnawed. If you find some, sit down nearby, in a place where you will have a good view of the tree, and remain still for twenty minutes or half an hour—though you may get a shot much sooner than that.

■ Do some bird listening. Blue jays, blackbirds and occasionally other species like to scold squirrels, thus revealing their location. A prolonged or repeated scolding bears investigation.

■ A favorite escape tactic of squirrels is simply to scurry around to the opposite side of a tree trunk or limb. If you follow, bushytail will continue girdling the wood, maintaining a solid shield. Instead, toss a stone or small fallen branch over to the far side and be ready to shoot. The noise produced when it lands will usually send your target around to your side of the tree.

■ When using rabbit hounds (beagles are deservedly the most popular breed for this sport), you should be carrying a shotgun because the shots will be at bounding targets. For hunting without dogs, you can use a shotgun or a rifle. A 12- or 20-gauge shotgun is recommended, with an improved cylinder or modified choke for brushy terrain, a full choke for long, open shots. High-velocity shells are best, with No. 6 shot for cottontails and 4, 5 or 6 for snowshoe rabbits or jacks. A rimfire rifle is good, either standard or magnum. Neither high-velocity cartridges nor hollow-points are really needed unless you want to test your marksmanship by taking only distant shots; many hunters prefer standard-velocity long rifle cartridges—or the superbly accurate long rifle match ammunition if they're going to confine themselves to tough head shots. The best sighting equipment for a rabbit rifle is a 2½X scope. As with squirrel hunting, the 5mm. rimfire magnum is a good substitute for the 22 in open, long-range country, with a scope of 2½X to 4X magnification.

■ Although hounds are used for jackrabbiting in the East, all you have to do is stroll about the typical jack terrain of the West or Southwest and you'll see plenty of targets. They go like the devil when they're going—offering exciting scatter gun targets—but they invariably pause after a few bounds. At that moment, they can be potted with an open-sighted 22 handgun or rifle, just as a cottontail or snowshoe can be at modest range.

■ The pads on the feet of rabbit hounds and coon hounds—and fox, cat or bear hounds, too, for that matter—can become very sore from hard running if they haven't been kept in tough condition by pre-season workouts. Some hunters apply a commercial pad conditioner to their dogs' paws. Others coat the pads with a mixture of tannic acid and pine tar, after which the paw is dipped in a pan or saucer of fuller's earth. This coating provides reliable protection.

■ A cottontail that appears to be fleeing at tremendous speed is really traveling only about twenty miles an hour, but the bounds and sudden hairpin switches of direction make the rabbit a tough target. Some experienced gunners who are determined to have *hasenpfeffer* for dinner time their gun swing and trigger pull so that they can hit the target during the brief moment between bounds or at the instant of landing. Some marksmen are good enough to do this with an open-sighted rifle instead of a shotgun. In such shooting, the trick is to handle the rifle like a shotgun—tracking the target smoothly and adding a pronounced follow-through as the trigger is pulled.

■ The snowshoe rabbit—more properly known as the varying hare—is marvelously equipped for its northern haunts. Not only does it have big, specially furred feet for traversing snow but it also changes from a brown camouflage coat in the summer to a snow white pelt in the winter. It can be almost invisible against snow. Almost. If you're a dogless hunter, follow the tracks and watch for the telltale dark eyes and black ear tips of your quarry.

■ If there are plenty of snowshoe rabbits in your area, it's a good time to hunt bobcats as well. The rabbits are the mainstay of the bobcat diet. The cats stay close to the food supply, and the populations of the two species fluctuate together. At the bottom of a cycle, in a poor rabbit year, bobcat hunting won't be good either—even with fine cat hounds. Besides, it's poor conservation to hunt them when their population is in a decline.

■ The tastiest, sportiest, most popular game rabbit is the cottontail—still America's number one game animal. The best hunting areas for it are in farm country where there are overgrown fencerows, thickets, grass clumps, run-down orchards, weed patches, windbreaks, outbuildings, shrubbery, pruning piles, brush, valley cornfields or other cropland, weedy stream banks, grassy ditches, brush piles and brushy edges between woods and field.

■ In cold weather or just after it, check for rabbits along sumac strips with heavy undergrowth. The bark has a high fat content which nourishes the cottontails during hungry periods of deep snow.

■ When beagles start a rabbit or when you jump one alone but don't manage to get off a shot, don't go galloping through the woods in pursuit. You won't keep up with either the hounds or a cottontail. Stay where you are. Cottontails select a small living and feeding area that seems safe to them, and they always return to the security of the familiar. This means that the quarry will probably circle back to where you found it before very long, and you can be there waiting.

■ If you're without a dog, you and a couple of friends can conduct an efficient rabbit drive—pretty much the way you'd stage a deer or pheasant drive. Simply form a line, with wide intervals between hunters, and walk abreast through likely fields and patches of cover. You'll probably walk up a few rabbits and you never know when you'll flush some other species. You might find anything from a bedded fox to upland birds (assuming the season is still open).

■ When you're trying to walk up rabbits, stop and look around once in a while. Then continue in a slightly different direction. Just as this tactic tends to make pheasants and grouse flush, it will also panic many a hidden rabbit into bolting.

■ When a rabbit is fleeing and you're not sure of a shot, try giving a few short, sharp whistles. This will sometimes cause a cottontail to stop momentarily, giving you a better chance to shoot. Frequently a sharp whistle will also make a woodchuck, hidden in tall grass while feeding, sit up straight on its haunches and offer a good target.

■ A mouth-operated predator call—which mimics the squeals of a frightened, injured rabbit—can be used to attract a large number of predatory species, including foxes, bobcats, coyotes and raccoons. A commercial call that emits a rather piercing scream is excellent in cottontail country, particularly in dense cover where you're trying to call predators at relatively short range. But for long-range calling, especially where jackrabbits are plentiful, choose a call with a sufficiently thick or long reed to emit a deeper tone.

■ After some calling practice (with realism rather than carrying power as the chief goal), you'll be able to vary the tone somewhat by the way you blow the call and cup your hands. When trying to toll in predators, be well concealed in a natural or constructed blind and begin with a low tone. Repeat the call at short intervals. If your fox, bobcat or other quarry comes into view but doesn't yet present an adequate target, switch to a high-pitched scream and be ready for the predator to charge straight at what he thinks is an easy meal.

■ Because bobcats kill by making a stealthy stalk and a last-moment pounce, they'll come to a call circuitously and cautiously until very close. Coyotes run down their prey. A coyote may respond to a call from a mile away, and his final approach may be a headlong run. Raccoons are closer to the cats than the coyotes in their behavior, and foxes are somewhere in between.

■ Traditionalists believe that snow helps in locating a fox, but it only helps in finding a trail and may even slow up the dogs.

■ When you are using hounds, it pays to be very familiar with the area in which you plan to hunt a fox. Since the direction of the chase is never really predictable, several hunters may take stands at the points they believe a hounded fox may cross. The only other profitable maneuver is to watch the hounds when you can and to keep listening to them when they're out of sight, mentally following the chase. Then you can hurry to the likeliest spot to intercept the fox if he circles. Sometimes he won't. Often a fox will run one-half to a mile ahead of a dog.

■ Obviously, hunting foxes with dogs is shotgun sport, but without hounds you have a choice of scatter gun or rifle—the rifle sometimes has an edge. Any chuck rifle close to 6mm. will do, and a 4X scope is recommended. Unless you're out just to ramble and gamble, start early in the morning when snow is on the ground. Learn to differentiate fox tracks from those of small dogs. Mazelike wandering fox tracks mean that the animal is (or was) hunting mice. Somewhat straighter and more purposeful are the tracks a fox makes when heading for a specific destination—a favored bedding spot for a morning rest. This will often be on a slight elevation, enabling the fox to nap fitfully, rising up once in a while to scan his back trail and then look around in other directions. When you're trying to spot a fox way at the other end of wide, weedy fields, binoculars will help. If you do spot one but a long-range shot is impossible, you'll have to stalk closer. Move when the animal's head is down or turned the other way. Crouch. Go quietly.

■ Raccoon hunting is done at night with hounds. You can wrap the dogs' collars with reflecting tape so that they'll show up well in the beam of your lamp.

131

■ When treeing coons with hounds, any open-sighted 22 rimfire rifle or handgun will do, but a rifle with a 2½X scope is better, with or without a predator call, because some shots may be at fairly long range. Nighttime predator calling, on the other hand, will get you close shots or none at all. Coon hunters seldom use shotguns because they want an undamaged pelt.

■ Since coons like water, good places to hunt for them are near ponds, streams or lakes. Such spots are particularly good on moonless nights. Wear a spelunking-style head lamp, tilted so that just the edge of the beam touches the ground. Although this will give you enough illumination to see the eyes of an incoming raccoon, it won't be low enough for the harsh light to spook the game.

■ A rifle for prairie-dog shooting should have a 6X or variable-power scope on it. If there are "dog towns" that haven't been heavily hunted in your area, you will probably be able to creep to within 150 yards of the burrows and get plenty of shots. For this you can use 50- or 55-grain bullets in a 222. But since most shooting at these small targets will be from somewhat greater distances, the hotter chuck cartridges are called for. The 17 and the 224 are other good choices. Additional recommendations would include the 222 magnum, the 223 and the 22-250.

■ Prairie dogs, eastern woodchucks and western rockchucks afford the best possible preseason practice for big-game hunting because they offer small targets, usually at long range. A rifleman who has mastered the techniques necessary for consistent hits will have no trouble hitting a target the size of the vital zone on big game (barring such variables as fatigue and buck fever). These techniques include not only a steady hold and a precise sight picture but also an accurate range and wind estimation. This kind of off-season practice is all the more valuable because it involves the same general type of rifle and sighting equipment—and sometimes the very same rifle and scope—that will be used later on big game. Finally, the extensive walking (and the frequent climbing in rockchuck regions) necessary to hunt these small animals helps to put a person into condition for a big-game hunt.

■ In lush farmlands where woodchucks abound, the animals can afford to be fussy about their diet. They like hay, alfalfa, succulent clover and luxuriant bluegrass. Knowing this, you can find the hot spots quickly and avoid barren areas.

■ When the hay is high, chuck hunting is difficult because you can't see them. Learn the farmers' harvesting cycle. The shooting is best during the first couple of weeks after a field has been trimmed.

■ There is no single "right" caliber for woodchuck hunting because the choice depends on average ranges and on the local tolerance for noise. Across wide pastures, meadows and fields, a relatively powerful, heavy, high-velocity, wind-bucking, low-trajectory cartridge is needed. Such shooting is generally done far enough from human habitation that a fairly loud rifle report won't be objectionable. Where farmhouses and other buildings are close together, you will need a quieter load for the sake of both people and domestic animals. The average range is also likely to be short enough for achieving fine accuracy with less-powerful cartridges. For distances up to at least 250 yards include the 222 magnum, the 223, the 220 Swift if you have a rifle chambered for it and the little 17, none of which is terribly noisy. Other recommendations for 300-yard-or-so precision shooting include the 22-250 Remington, the 25-06 and the 270 Winchester. For moderate distances, a couple of heavier-bullet loads, the 280 Remington and the 30-06, are good and so are the powerful modern chamberings that stretch accuracy to ranges as long as 450 yards—the 25-06 Remington (based on a wonderful old "wildcat" cartridge), the 243 Winchester, the 6mm. Remington and the 6.5mm. Remington.

■ At comparable ranges, the calibers listed above for woodchucks are also excellent for hunting western species—prairie dogs, rockchucks and coyotes. The heftier calibers in the list (those in the 6mm. and 25 class) are also excellent for hunting pronghorn antelope, deer, sheep and goats—one more reason that hunting the small animals is recommended preparation for hunting the larger species.

■ For hunting woodchucks and similar animals at ranges up to about 200 yards, a 6X or 8X scope is more than sufficiently powerful. At 200 to 300 yards, 8X or 10X is plenty. If the ranges are likely to vary considerably, a 3X to 9X or a 2X to 10X variable scope is good. For very long range shooting, 12X is recommended. The higher-powered, target-type scopes are optically superb but are

133

relatively long, heavy, expensive, sometimes fragile and more difficult to use. Nevertheless, they are unbeatable if your hunting style is rather sedentary and if you can practice sufficiently to overcome the magnification of visual wavering that accompanies great sight-picture enlargement.

■ For long-range shooting, you will find a bipod or other portable rifle rest a great help. Some shooters are also aided by the range-estimating devices that are built into the reticles of certain scope models.

■ If you're hunting chucks or similar animals on foot, go slowly and do lots of looking. Always carry binoculars. (Some shooters also use spotting scopes.) Thoroughly glass all likely looking fields or pastures. If you cruise the back roads in a car, watch not only for chucks but for land pocked with their holes. When you find a target, choose a shooting site that offers a clear shot, preferably from the prone position, and check where your bullet will travel in the event of a miss.

■ The two closely related species of marmot known as rockchucks are both found in greatest numbers on the slopes of the Rockies, from Alberta all the way down to New Mexico. Look for them around outcroppings and rock slides adjacent to grassy meadows. The hot spots are usually near or above timberline, seldom much below it. As with big game, search for signs—but instead of droppings, tracks and rubbings you'll be looking for the mounds of earth at den mouths. If there's no chuck in sight when you spot a den colony, stalk up close enough for a good shot anyway. Then settle down and wait. Before long, a chuck may well emerge from one of the burrows.

■ For the type of moderate-range shooting described above, the

5mm. Remington rimfire magnum is excellent, though for ranges beyond 150 yards, you should go to one of the centerfire chuck cartridges mentioned earlier. The 5mm. cartridge is loaded with Power-Lokt bullets, which are excellent for this kind of hunting. With the centerfire chuck calibers, too, you should use Power-Lokt or similar bullets, which deliver pinpoint accuracy. Be sure that rising ground provides a backstop between you and any habitation, road, etc. And never shoot in the direction of buildings.

■ Whether you're hunting eastern woodchucks or western rock-chucks, take along a beginner—a youngster, for instance, who's eager to learn. The 5mm. rimfire magnum, with a 4X scope, is perfect for the neophyte. It has low noise, little recoil and fine accuracy, and it handles easily. Moreover, both the rifle and the ammunition for it are inexpensive.

■ There is a universal tendency to hold too high when making a long shot at an angle off the horizontal. This is true whether the shot is uphill or downhill. If you find yourself missing more than normally when hunting in rockchuck country, which requires you to shoot on slopes, try holding a little low.

■ The most common mistake made among crow hunters who use scatter guns is selecting oversized shot pellets. Regardless of what you may have heard or read, crows are not at all hard to bring down *if* you give yourself the dense-pattern advantage of small shot. Skeet loads of No. 9 are excellent, and there's rarely any reason to use sizes larger than No. 8. A 12-gauge shotgun with a modified choke is ideal.

■ Although shotguns are most often used for crow hunting, a rifle is fine when you aim only at birds on the ground or—assuming there's an adequately safe backstop—in low branches. Any standard or high-speed 22 rimfire, the 5mm. rimfire magnum or even one of the smaller centerfire chuck calibers will be very effective over the ranges at which you can spot and aim at crows. A 4X scope would be a good choice of sighting equipment, but if you happen to have a chuck rifle with a 6X scope, that's fine, too.

■ Every spring and autumn, great flocks of migrating crows tend to return to the same roosts of the previous year and remain there for several nights or even weeks before continuing their migration. Even during the summer, sizable concentrations may stay on at the same sites. One key to good crow shooting is to scout the country-side—listening as well as looking—for these roosting areas.

■ Until crows fly quite close to your blind, remain crouched so that the sight of your head won't give you away. Most hunters wear camouflage clothing and hats. Some also wear face nets or masks or smear their faces with mud or lampblack for better concealment.

■ To perfect your crow calling, listen to live birds as often as you can and buy a few calling records. You'll find that these birds have a large, sophisticated vocabulary, with different calls to signal danger, food, a fight, a wish to gather, etc. Though it's legal to use phonographic calls for actual hunting—and many gunners do—it's sportier to perfect your technique with a mouth call. Expert crow hunters also claim that it's more effective when done proficiently because the caller can switch instantly to any sound desired, depending on the situation. Some gunners keep two calls on a neck cord, each with a slightly different tone, for greater versatility.

■ Crow decoys are very effective when propped in tree branches. You can also set out a few on the ground some distance from the blind, imitating feeding birds. A gathering and feeding call is appropriate to this setup.

■ A decoy variation is the crow-and-owl rig. Owls and crows are implacable enemies—it is for this reason that commercial owl decoys are available. Prop one owl on a low branch or on the ground, with several crows higher up and surrounding it as if they were ganging up on him. The appropriate call is the bullying and fighting sound. If you've never heard this racket, use a commercial call record to get the hang of it. The crows will immediately come to investigate.

Medium-
and Big-
Game Hunting

The term *big game* is a bit hard to define because it has been loosely (and traditionally) applied to so many animals. To avoid confusion, many authorities divide into two categories—*medium* and big game—all those furred animals that are obviously larger than small game. There is general agreement that the medium classification includes pronghorn antelope, whitetail deer, mountain goats and sheep and the collared peccary, or javelina, of the Southwest. Big-game species include the wild boar, the mule deer, the bear, the elk, the caribou and the moose.

Most kinds of big-game hunting share certain common elements. For example, with the exception of whitetail deer in some states and occasionally wild boar, all the species are generally hunted with rifled arms rather than shotguns. In most cases a relatively powerful scope-sighted rifle is used. And regardless of which species is the quarry (or primary quarry), hunters making trips into unfamiliar regions usually hire a guide or guide-outfitter.

■ To obtain a list of licensed guides and guide-outfitters, write to the game commission of the state (or Canadian province) where you plan to hunt. Inquire at the same time about obtaining a nonresident big-game hunting license, special permits and permit drawings for particular species where required. Do this as far in advance of the planned hunt as possible. Some nonresident licenses and permits must be obtained a year or more in advance of the season because they are issued on a first-come, first-served basis. And there are guides who are booked up for a full year, too.

■ Write to several guides in the desired area and ask about their prices and usual arrangements. Some may send brochures with full particulars, while others will send less-formal replies. Be sure to get all pertinent information—including prospects for the game you want during the upcoming season. Even more important, ask for references and then check those references. Finally, once you've chosen your guide, get from him an explicit written statement listing what equipment he will supply and what you are to bring, any suggestions he has regarding arms and ammunition, exactly where and when you are to meet, what (if any) transportation is included in his fee, where you will hunt and for how long.

■ Follow the guide's suggestions—not only those he makes in advance but those he gives you during the hunt. A guide earns his good references and repeat business by knowing where and how to hunt big game, how to get along safely and enjoyably in the wilderness—and how to judge whether a trophy that looks gigantic to you will be disappointing in comparison with the next game you spot.

■ When planning a guideless hunt, study a topographical map, checking for trails, waterways, landmarks and game-harboring features, such as brushy canyons or valleys where browse and good cover would attract animals and higher ridges where they would bed down. Also look for passes and other natural "funnels" likely to be used by moving game. Carry the map with you on the hunt, and also carry a compass. Even in familiar territory, check your bearings.

■ Whether you're on stand or hunting through likely cover or glassing the surrounding terrain, it's unusual to spot an entire animal (except for goats or sheep on distant crags or pronghorns and occasionally mule deer in very open country). A traditional white-tail-hunting technique often works with other species as well: Scan the cover carefully, looking for *parts* of a concealed animal—the oblong, horizontal, solid-colored splotch of a buck's side, the light or sometimes white patch of brisket or belly, the dark, round eye, the smoothly outlined tan ear among more jagged shapes of brush. A tree branch that curves too smoothly or glints in the sun or moves may be an antler. A sapling that doesn't look quite right may be a leg. Watch for movement. The twitch of an ear may reveal your trophy. The perception of movement is important not only while hunting in dense cover but also when glassing distant terrain where game colors blend with the background.

■ Learn the anatomy of the game you're after and the vital areas where a shot must be placed for a quick, clean hit. It is always far better to pass up a chance at game than to wound and lose an animal. In general, neck shots are excellent for medium and large game. Also excellent (and often an easier target) is the heart-lung area—the entire forward chest, from just above the foreleg upward to a few inches below the spine. If you shoot for the center or lower center of this target, a bullet that misses the heart will probably strike the lungs—and vice versa. Even if both of these vital organs are missed, breaking down this shoulder area will usually cause the animal to drop quickly and a fast finishing shot can then be made. A spinal shot also brings immediate collapse, but it is too difficult a shot to try unless the range is short and you're an expert. Do not place any shot rear of the chest.

■ When stalking game, move while the animal's head is turned away from you or—preferably—down to feed. Even if you don't think you're in the open from the animal's vantage point, freeze when game puts its head up or your quarry is likely to bolt before you can aim. Once you're close enough, continue to move very slowly as you bring the rifle up and be as silent as possible.

■ When you are prowling the rim of a brush-choked draw or canyon, your best bet may be to spook the game purposely, forcing the animal to come into view while "topping out" over the rim to escape. If you have a partner, work one man through the draw, pushing the game out ahead of him as in a deer drive so that the other man can get a shot. When hunting alone, try tossing stones down into the draw or even pepper the cover with a slingshot.

■ For close-range hunting in thick timber, some hunters prefer an open or aperture sight instead of a scope. This can be helpful for making quick, close shots. However, if you think the light is going to be dim and your front sight is black, you can facilitate aiming by spotting the bead or top of the post with white chalk, lacquer or enamel. You may find it helpful to outline a rear notch in the same way. Conversely, on sunny days you may want to *blacken* your sights. A small piece of birch bark carried in your pocket is good for this purpose. Just burn it and pass the sight through the thick, dark smoke.

■ In most areas, a scope is better than iron sights, even when the cover is fairly thick. Such cover calls for a low-powered scope, of course, and fairly coarse crosshairs or a post reticle that shows up well and can be used quickly. At one time, scopes only added to the difficulties of hunting in poor light, but the good modern ones actually *gather* light.

■ Big game can be dangerous when it appears quite dead. Antlers and hooves have been known to flail even when the eyes were glassy. It is best to approach fallen game from the rear, watching for signs of life and ready to shoot again. Jab the hindquarters sharply with a branch or your rifle. If there is any movement, fire a finishing shot. If not, circle around to the front for a look at the eyes. A good finishing shot is one placed through the spinal cord in the lower neck; this is quick and will not damage a trophy or waste large edible portions.

■ Just as cottontail rabbits are America's most popular small game, whitetail deer are America's number one big (or medium) game. But deer are much smarter than rabbits and rely much more heavily on their sense of smell to detect danger. Here are some ways to avoid alerting whitetails to your presence even when thick timber requires short-range stalking or ambushing: If you live on a farm or have a friend who farms, wear "barn clothes" or hang your hunting clothes in a barn for a couple of days and then hang them outdoors for another day before hunting. Lacking a barn, hang the clothes outdoors for a couple of days, preferably near or among evergreen trees, to get rid of the human scent. Just before hunting, briskly rub your clothes with a fresh balsam or pine bough. Still doubtful about your aroma? Spray your clothes (but don't overdo it) with a pine-scented air freshener or cedar oil. That takes care of your clothes but not you. Make yourself less offensive to deer by not using hair tonic, scented soap or shaving lotion before you hunt; their odors are alien, and therefore frightening, to deer. Incidentally, these precautions are even more important to bow hunters than to riflemen and shotgunners because a bow hunter should never attempt a shot except at extremely short range.

■ There are differences of opinion about the effectiveness of commercial deer scents. Many successful deer hunters never use them, but on the other hand it's better to smell like a deer (or almost anything else) than like a human being—at least when you're hunting whitetails. Apply the stuff sparingly, however. If you don't have the commercial deer lure and another member of your party has killed his deer, you can use the real thing instead of store-bought scent. Just rub the scent glands of a freshly dressed deer on your boots and boot soles.

■ A good substitute for deer lure, if you don't like its odor, is ordinary oil of anise or anise flavoring. Although it doesn't smell like a deer to a deer, it does mask human scent, and its odor is somewhat like that of fermenting apples, which deer love. Drugstores sell oil of anise, and many supermarkets sell anise flavoring.

■ Hunting deer from a stand is most effective from dawn to mid-morning when deer are ambling up the slopes from their nocturnal feeding areas to their higher, more-concealed bedding grounds and again in late afternoon when they filter down to feed. Good stands are along beechnut flats and ridges, the edges of apple orchards, near cedars, pines, firs, hemlocks, sumac or good falls of white acorns—or near a well-used deer run that is easily recognizable from the tracks. Station yourself a little distance from the run so that you'll be able to see the deer in enough time to get a broadside shot. Another good location is wherever saplings show plenty of buck rubs—scars marking places where deer have polished their antlers. Try to be stationed higher than where the deer will be, for deer seldom look for danger from above. This is the reason that tree stands are often used.

■ Driving is a good way to hunt relatively small patches of woods, thick swamps, islands of brush and the like. As many as fifty hunters sometimes join forces in a drive, but a smaller party (half-a-dozen to a dozen-and-a-half hunters) would be better for most types of cover. Since a driving plan is important, choose a leader who is familiar enough with the terrain that he can station standers and direct the drivers. The standers should be posted at points from which they're safe from anyone else's gunfire, yet they should still have a good view of any deer that filter out. For safety's sake, they must stay put until the drive is over. A line of drivers, placed 50 to 100 yards apart, now moves forward through the cover to drive deer toward the standers. Some drives are silent because all it takes to move deer is the movement of the hunters through the woods. Other drives involve talking and even whistling to get the game moving, but too much noise is ineffective. The object is to make the deer just nervous enough to move out. If they panic, they may come out too fast to allow for a good shot or they may double back or they may manage to sneak past the standers—a trick at which they are adept.

■ In large hunting areas, particularly mountainous ones, the most productive way to find deer is probably just to walk slowly and silently, heading upwind and pausing frequently to look around and listen. Look at your backtrail, too, as timid but inquisitive deer will sometimes come out behind you.

■ Still another hunting method, which seems to be most popular in the Southwest, is "rattling" for bucks. It is used during the rutting season to imitate the sound of two bucks fighting. This will often attract a real buck. It is done from a hiding place, of course—a good stand near a deer run or area marked with buck rubs. The equipment consists of a cut-apart pair of antlers, preferably heavy-beamed. You slam them together, mimicking bucks charging at each other, and then rattle and scrape and twist them to and fro, imitating the subsequent horn-locking, jockeying and thrusting.

■ If you hunt whitetails in areas where it is legal to use only rifled slugs (or buckshot), you should be armed with a 12-gauge magnum shotgun. A repeater is best, and it should be equipped with a low-powered scope or at least rifle-type sights. Even double-barreled guns can be equipped with screw-on or clip-on rifle-type sights, which will slightly improve their accuracy for hunting big game. A shotgun should not be used on deer at much over sixty yards.

■ For whitetail hunting in timber, recommended calibers include the 6mm., the 243, the 6.5mm., the 30-30, the 308 and the 35 Remington. For open country or mixed terrain, good choices are the 6.5mm., the 25-06, the 7mm. magnum, the 270, the 280 and the 300 magnums. These calibers are also fine for other game shot at relatively long range—antelope, mule deer, sheep, goats. In addition to these, the venerable 30-06 is good, regardless of terrain. A 2½X scope is fine for whitetail hunting in wooded areas; a 4X or variable-power scope is best for whitetails or mule deer in open country. A variable such as 2X to 7X is suitable for all types of deer hunting.

■ From any vantage point or stand, find more than one area to watch. Deer are not always predictable; besides, if the wind changes, you'll be downwind of a different area. Stay concealed, but clear a spot for your feet so that you won't snap twigs and crunch dry leaves. Also make sure you have room to move your rifle and an opening through which to aim and shoot. Be sure of your target.

■ The best whitetail hot spots change as the season progresses. At first the animals seem to stay in the woods to a great extent, but later they appear in the fields more often—in alfalfa fields, cornfields and apple orchards.

■ A deer tag that's been attached through the gambrel can sometimes pull out and be lost while you're dragging your game out. To avoid this, wrap a handkerchief or scarf around it and tie securely.

■ Mule deer are somewhat more migratory than whitetails, and they head for warmer—lower—country as the weather gets colder. Since they follow pretty much the same migration routes year after year, do your hunting along one of these trails when the cold begins to drive them downward.

■ Because mule deer are creatures of habit and are subjected to less hunting pressure than whitetails, open season doesn't much change their daily routine. Preseason scouting should give you an idea of where they'll be at a given time of day.

143

■ The notion that mule deer are stupid is incorrect. They simply tend to count on distance rather than concealment as a protection because they are found in more-open country than whitetails. It pays to scan the middle and far distance for mule deer, using binoculars. If you can spot an animal far enough away that your presence is unsuspected, planning a stalk will be easier.

■ When a mule deer flees, he will generally try to head uphill. Chances are he's not very frightened and, being of an inquisitive species, he's very likely to pause and look back as he approaches a crest or any protective cover, giving you an excellent chance for a shot if you've gotten into position.

■ During the warm part of the day, mule deer like to bed on a shady, protected slope or ridge from which they have a view of the terrain below. The thermal currents rising along the slopes also help them scent danger. At this time, work along the ridges, glassing the land just below. You're not as likely to be seen or scented if you're above the animals, and you'll have a good view.

■ Because antelope inhabit prairies and deserts, they show up quite well even at long distance. But the herds post a sentinel—usually an old doe standing on a little rise. Watch her. If you can stalk to within range without letting her see you, you're likely to get a shot at a buck.

■ To keep some screening elevation between you and the game, pronghorns often must be stalked circuitously. Take your time, stay low and make your circle a big one. If you can get to within, say, two hundred or two hundred fifty yards and assume a prone position, you're in a good position.

■ You may not be able to get quite that close to your pronghorn. When you're as near as possible, gamble. Get into position, but stay hidden. Then raise your hat or handkerchief into view and gently wave it. (Indians used to decoy these curious animals by flagging them in a similar manner.) If it can't see that the object is being waved by a human being, it will sometimes make a cautious approach. Lower your arm slowly and quietly, and be ready to shoot. This method sometimes works with another inquisitive animal—the caribou.

■ If a band of antelope spooks, stay in position and be ready to shoot. They're usually moving too fast and are too far away to risk a running shot, but a buck will generally bring up the rear—herding his does away from danger—and will frequently stop and look back after running a short distance.

■ Sheep and goats are high-mountain animals. Vital equipment for hunting them includes tough but comfortable boots, good lungs, strong legs—and no fear of heights. They offer the toughest kind of hunting in America, and the climb is the most difficult part. A couple of months before a mountain hunt, you should have a medical checkup and begin to condition yourself. Training should include long walks, hikes on difficult terrain, climbing and jogging.

■ For hunting sheep or goats, you will also need a pair of 7X or 8X binoculars and a 20X spotting scope (sometimes your guide will provide that). The binoculars are for scanning far-off crags and mountain meadows. The spotting scope is for a closer look at a potential trophy head. With goats, the difference between poor horns and good ones is a matter of just a couple of inches of length. When you are deciding whether to shoot or whether to search farther, you need to rely on the spotting scope and the advice of your guide. With sheep, you're looking for a large, full-curl set of horns. The horns may be broomed (broken off); if the brooming is severe, uneven or on only one side, you may not want the trophy. Or the curl may simply look better than it is to a naked or inexperienced eye.

■ Sheep and goats have incredibly good eyesight and an excellent sense of smell. However, since they're accustomed to hearing stones roll down the slopes, you can often get within range if you can work with the wind, stay concealed and are careful about making unnatural noises, such as clicking a rifle bolt. Because both species look for danger from below and escape predators by climbing, the trick is to get high up and stalk from above.

■ The European wild boar, which was introduced in this country over two generations ago, can now be hunted in a number of states —notably in Tennessee and North Carolina, where the hogs long ago established themselves in the mountainous woods, and in New Hampshire and California, where they were introduced on preserves much more recently but have fared very well. Feral hogs and domestic-wild crosses have also become plentiful in Florida and Texas. State game commissions can furnish names of guides or preserve managers. They generally work with a pack of well-trained hounds.

■ For hunting the big European wild boar, you will need a powerful repeater—something on the order of a 308, a 350 Remington, a 30-06, a 35 Remington or a 7mm. Remington magnum. You will need at least a 175-grain bullet or, better yet, a 200-grain. Some of the Appalachian guides use 30-30 lever actions, but they have more experience and skill than the average hunter. Because the range will be short when you catch up to the hounds and the boar, open sights are used. For this reason, some hunters use 12-gauge shotguns with rifled slugs.

■ Short range is also the rule with hunting the smaller feral hogs. They are sometimes hunted with handguns—a 357, a 41 or a 44 magnum. You can also use a shotgun slug or a medium-powered rifle, again with open sights.

■ Many hunters think of the caribou as being indigenous to Alaska, the Yukon and the Northwest Territories. A trip to caribou country therefore seems exceedingly expensive to people living in the eastern half of the United States. The fact is that either woodland or barren-ground caribou can be found throughout most of Canada. Write to the game department of the nearest province if you have a yearning to go after this trophy. For easterners, a particularly good area is the Ungava region of Quebec, midway between Hudson Bay and the southern tip of Greenland. In this region, it is possible to arrange to stay at a commercial camp that offers excellent salmon and trout fishing as well as fine hunting. Northern Ontario also has caribou and is, of course, noted for moose and other big game.

■ Caribou often come to water in early morning and late afternoon. Look for them at these times along streams. Their feed consists chiefly of tundra mosses and lichens, and they prefer to bed on open hilltops, gravelly ridges or snow patches.

■ Shots at caribou must sometimes be made at long range, but the animals do not seem to have as much resistance to shock as other large species. (Actually, they're not as big as they look when their great antlers are silhouetted above a ridge; a good buck is likely to weigh only three hundred pounds.) You need an accurate, medium-power rifle. Anything that is used for sheep or goats would be fine, and a 4X scope is suggested. Both males and females have antlers—unlike any other North American deer species—but those of the female are unimpressive. Still, trophy judgment can be difficult because even a mediocre buck is awe-inspiring at first sight. Your guide will advise you whether the trophy is a good one; don't shoot without his approval.

■ Although bears are most often shot as incidental bonuses, hunting specifically for them is still a popular sport. Any rifle adequate for mule deer will be more than sufficient for black bears—a 7mm. Remington magnum or a 30-06 is fine—and the best shot for any bear species is in the neck or lower chest. Scoping requirements depend on terrain and hunting method. There are regions—particularly in western Canada—where shots must be made across wide tidal flats, tundra or grasslands at forest edges; this may call for a 4X scope. In woodlands, however, 2½X is plenty. Grizzlies should not be hunted anywhere in the United States, regardless of state laws, because they are too scarce. But there are parts of Canada where they are relatively numerous. A good caliber for them would be the 7mm. Remington magnum, one of the 300 magnums, the 30-06 or the 350 Remington magnum, and a 4X scope is advisable. The last-named caliber, with the same scope power, is the best for the great brown bear (sometimes erroneously called the Kodiak bear) of northwestern Canada and Alaska.

■ The best method of bear hunting is to locate droppings, tracks and rubbings, indicating that a spot is frequented by one or more bears, and then take a concealed stand and wait. In grizzly country, another sign to look for are long gashes clawed in the bark of a tree.

■ For skinning out a bear, sharpen your knife to a steep bevel on only one side. Use the knife with the beveled side down to get through the thick fat, right down to the hide.

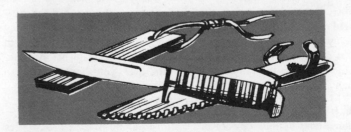

■ Even with the right kind of knife, dressing and skinning a bear (or any other big game) is a task that demands skill if you are to avoid ruining either meat or trophy. If you're on a first hunt for any species, let the guide do the dressing and/or skinning. This is part of his job, and he expects to do it. But watch him carefully, and ask him about any step you don't understand so that you'll be able to do it properly if you're ever hunting alone for the same species.

■ Theoretically, there are two types of loads for elk, or wapiti. In the "brush-busting" class (for heavy forest), such cartridges as the 350 Remington magnum and the 375 H&H magnum are frequently listed. For long-range shooting in more-open country, the listings include the 270, the 280, the 7mm. Remington magnum, the 30-06, the 300 magnums (Winchester and H&H) and, again, the 350 magnum. But even in forested terrain, a long shot may well be needed to reach a bull elk on one of the open meadows where the animals like to feed. One of the long-range calibers and a scope power of 2 ½ X to 4X would be the best choice.

■ Elk are generally hunted by stalking, tracking and—in the rutting season—calling. In spite of the popularity of the term *bugling*, the call is more like a high-pitched whistle. It is imitated with a mouth-operated call (a metal, plastic, rubber or wooden pipe) that is quite difficult to use realistically. Since silence is preferable to poor calling, this should be done only by an experienced guide or a hunter who is thoroughly familiar with elk.

■ The elk hunter should work high ridges in the early morning and again in the late afternoon, trying to stay above the quarry. Another good method is to take a stand in a basin where there is a good view of the slopes and glass for bedded or standing bulls.

■ At dawn, elk begin to move from wooded cover near the timberline out to places where they can graze and browse. They particularly like aspen leaves and twigs. In the early morning, they enjoy feeding on sunny slopes, but they'll return to dense forest to rest during the noon hours, coming out to feed again before dusk. Since they use the same trails over and over, you should be able to find a likely spot from which to glass their habitat.

■ It is common to jump bedded elk in thick timber at noontime. Sometimes hunters on foot are stationed along likely escape routes while others ride through the area on horseback to drive bulls into the open.

■ When tracking an elk on snow, don't just walk along in the tracks. The elk, like most big game, will occasionally check the back trail and is likely to sense your presence. Parallel the trail, along higher ground if possible, or make a wide circle to try an interception play.

■ Moose are, generally speaking, easier to locate than a good bull elk and are taken at relatively moderate ranges. However, because of their size and stamina, you need a rifle delivering plenty of energy. Good choices include the 30-06, the 7mm. magnum, the 300 magnums and the 350 magnum. For eastern hunting, a 2½X scope is recommended; in the West, a 4X scope is better because shots made in the Rockies or western Canada are almost always 200 yards or more. By contrast, shots made along the eastern waterways and swamps may be at any range from 30 paces to 150.

■ In many areas, the moose season opens in late summer—before rutting begins. The meat is then at its best, but calling is useless. You must know the animal's habits in order to locate a trophy bull (or a cow if you're more interested in table fare and if it is legal to hunt them). Moose prefer to feed on willow, aspen and birch browse, plus lily roots and a few other aquatic plants. Look for boggy meadows, cranberry bogs, aspen and willow thickets and waters rich in plant life.

■ A popular eastern moose-hunting method, for both searching and stalking, is to move along a waterway silently in a canoe. But if your guide forgets to warn you about deep water, bear in mind that even an eastern moose may weigh twelve hundred pounds or more. An animal of that size can be nearly impossible to wrestle ashore if he has been taken in deep, muddy-bottomed water. The guide will handle the canoe while you get ready with your rifle. Don't shoot until he tells you to. He may spook the moose intentionally at the last moment to make the animal head for shore. At short range, you can hit a moving moose without much difficulty, and subsequent tasks will be much easier if he falls near or on shore.

■ In the West, moose are hunted on horseback. You ride from mountain meadow to mountain meadow, making sure to glass each likely spot *before* you ride out of the concealing timber. If you spot your game, dismount and move slowly, stalking upwind and above the animal.

■ Moose are sometimes easy to track on snow or soft ground. Before bedding down, the animal will often swing around—into the wind—for a reassuring look at the back trail. If you suspect this is happening, move crosswind off the track. If the track begins to zig-zag, the moose is probably looking for a bedding spot—you'll either have a shot soon or spook the animal out of sight. Now you're not just tracking but stalking. Look for coniferous or brushy pockets where your trophy may be bedded.

■ As in elk hunting, calling is often effective in attracting moose during the rut. A birch-bark horn—in essence, a megaphone—is used. And as in elk hunting, it must be used well or it will merely scare away all game. Unless your guide wants to take the time to teach you the technique (and unless you prove to be an apt student), leave the calling to him. He may put you on stand while he calls, or he may call while exploring in a canoe. Calling seems to work best in the East, on or near water. A moose accepting the challenge of the call may come crashing out of the woods at close range, but it is more likely that you'll hear an answering call and then the movements of approach first. Just remain quiet and be ready to make a careful, safe shot.

Upland Birds
and
Waterfowl

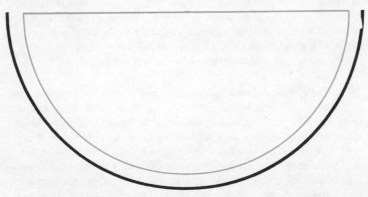

Only the hunter who perceives every upland flush and every incoming wildfowl flight as a new experience, fraught with new possibilities, will be sufficiently alert to limit out consistently. Those who base their actions on preconceptions of "average" game behavior often fail to notice the game-getting exceptions that prove the game-getting rules. A successful hunter must, of course, learn from experience. And although hunting techniques that work with one species can often be used to bag another, each species merits individual study and respect.

■ Many ringneck pheasants are missed because of insufficient lead or failure to follow through on the swing—or because the long tail feathers make the target look bigger than it really is. Concentrate on only the forward portion of the bird, disregarding the rear "false-target" end. To avoid hitting the bird with an overly dense pattern, thus spoiling a potential game dinner, it's also best to wait out a shot until the bird has towered and leveled off—but at that point you must no longer think of the bird as a slowpoke, since the pheasant is misleadingly fast. The ideal range for this and most other upland species is between twenty and forty yards.

■ Bobwhite quail *seem* faster than ringnecks, but they're not even making forty miles an hour as they streak out of a field. Their small size and explosive flush may give an appearance of greater speed. Concentrate on swinging the gun with one bird and you'll generally find you have more time for a good shot than you would have supposed. You will frequently even have time for a double on one flush.

■ Doves, believe it or not, are not much faster than bobwhites in usual flight. But their flight is erratic, sometimes as fast as sixty miles an hour, and often high, so you must be quick about sweeping the muzzle through the target area, with plenty of follow-through to spray the shot pattern across the flight path.

■ Ruffed grouse are slower. The difficulty here is the combination of frequent surprise flushes and the grouse habit of dodging behind trees and foliage. A bird that seems to be flying with tremendous speed may be covering only a short distance quickly before being hidden by screening woods. The vital technique here is not a long lead but a really fast swing—often snap shooting or semisnap shooting. Woodcock are downright slow by comparison, but their erratic, corkscrewing flushes are disconcerting. The trick with a woodcock is to wait it out if the cover permits, letting the bird level off, and then shoot fast before intervening cover blots out the little target.

■ Anyone who has watched a puppy "sight pointing" knows that the canine reaction to visual stimuli comes earlier than the reaction to scent. For early training sessions, let the dog see what it's all about by using a bird wing of the desired species. Using an old fishing rod, attach it to a line and cast it out near the dog. Then move it a little by manipulating the rod or reeling in a bit to get the student's attention. With a retriever, an even more effective attention-getter is a tennis ball with feathers glued to it. Almost every dog loves the toss-and-fetch game, so just toss the ball a short distance and let the dog bring it back to you.

■ Some shotgunners improve their shooting by using one type of gun for all hunting so that they can become thoroughly accustomed to a particular model's action, balance and handling qualities. But there's the problem of needing a different gauge and/or barrel length and choke for some kinds of hunting. An obvious solution is to buy several editions of the same model, but there are less expensive approaches. One is to choose a model for which interchangeable barrels are available. With some models—the Remington pumps and autos come to mind—it's possible to buy two guns of different gauges but with the same design, each with interchangeable barrels providing a choice of length and choke. In effect, this can provide you with a whole battery of shotguns for hunting (and for clay targets) without spending a huge sum or sacrificing the one-model idea.

■ In both upland hunting and duck hunting, it's a common mistake to use too much barrel and too much choke. Few gunners seem to realize that the average range at which they shoot quail and woodcock is only about twenty yards, and most other upland game is brought down at no more than perhaps thirty yards. A short, quick-swinging, open-choked barrel is needed for such shooting; a length of twenty-six inches, with an improved-cylinder choke, is a much better choice than a longer, tighter bore. Likewise, many wildfowlers seem unaware that a twenty-eight-inch barrel with a modified choke is excellent both for jump shooting and for close-range ducking over decoys. The traditional thirty-inch full-choke duck-and-goose barrel is great for pass shooting and for long-range gunning over decoys—usually on big waters—but it is actually a detriment in most other types of hunting.

■ Another common error is to "compensate" for the use of a small gauge by using a large shot size. Theoretically, larger shot delivers more energy per pellet, but it's far more important to have the dense pattern provided by a smaller shot size. To get more power you can switch to heavier charges—even three-inch magnums if your gun is chambered for them—but base your shot size on the game and type of hunting you plan to do rather than on gauge. Here's a handy guide to recommended shot sizes: No. 9 for woodcock, shorebirds and quail; 8 or 9 for grouse, woodcock, doves and quail; 7½ or 8 for chukars, quail, doves and pigeons; 7½ for grouse, Hungarian partridge, sharptails, quail, doves, woodcock, prairie chickens and ptarmigan; 6 for pheasants in open cover, for sharptails and prairie chickens late in the season and for short-range jump shooting or decoying of puddle ducks; 5 for pond and river ducks when pass shooting and for open-water ducks over decoys; 4 or 5 for brant; 4 for open-water ducks when pass shooting and for geese most of the time; 2 for high pass shooting at Canada geese and 2 or BB for turkey. There's one important exception to these guidelines: When you're hunting ducks over shallow water or mud flats where the birds may pick up fallen pellets and swallow them for "grit," don't use anything smaller than No. 5's, which are heavy enough to sink quickly out of reach. Too many small pellets may be swallowed by the ducks, causing lead poisoning.

■ Where the water is deep, fallen shot is not likely to be swallowed by ducks, and you may therefore want to carry a few extra shells loaded with No. 7½'s or even smaller pellets.

■ Watch your ducks when they fall. If a duck's head is down on the water, you or your dog should have little trouble retrieving the bird. But if the head is up, deliver a finishing shot quickly to avoid losing a cripple. When injured, some species can dive repeatedly or remain submerged for some time and others can paddle out of sight. Even when they fall on land, they should be marked down carefully and retrieved quickly. Crippled birds cannot survive, and there is no excuse for carelessly wasting game.

■ Upland birds should also be marked down carefully and retrieved immediately. For this purpose a dog is a great asset, but even a good dog will occasionally have trouble finding a bird in thick cover. If you have difficulty locating fallen game, next time watch it all the way down and scrape a line with your boot heel pointing toward it. (If several members of a party do this, you'll have a helpful crossbearing.) Before you blunder into the brush looking for your bird, prop your hat or hang your handkerchief at the spot where you made the shot. Then, if you don't find the bird on the first try, you can go back to the exact point from which you fired, facing in the direction indicated by your scraped boot mark, and try again.

■ Most misses are caused by using too little lead, rarely by too much. If you find yourself missing consistently, try increasing your lead. With waterfowl, you may have to go as far as doubling your lead. If you still have difficulty, it may pay—particularly with waterfowl and pheasants—to concentrate on only the head as a target. That way, if your lead is still a trifle short, you will have a better chance of scoring a clean body hit nonetheless.

■ Early in the hunting season, pheasants prefer to roost in dense cover, such as brush, high weed patches or swampy tangles, but by sunup they move to the feeding fields via ditches, fencerows and the like. Late in the morning or by noon, they'll look for shady resting, dusting and gravel-picking spots. Later in the afternoon, they'll feed again before returning to roost. You can choose your hunting area according to the time of day. Since the birds are more wary while feeding than while resting, it's best to hunt with a party, or at least a partner, during feeding periods. A good method is to have drivers comb a field, working toward two or more hunters stationed at the far end. Hunt away from, not toward, any bordering swamps or woods, and keep going to the very end of the field because ringnecks would rather make a sneak run than fly. As the season progresses, cold weather and food scarcity will change the birds' habits. Now they'll roost in heavier brush and swamps. Feeding periods will be longer and will often take place on the lee side of heavy cover. Resting periods will be spent on sun-warmed ground —not in shady spots—where the cover is relatively sparse. The long feeding periods will be near thick cover patches, through which a man or dog can work while several hunters surround the brushy area. If you hunt without a dog, walk very slowly and pause often to panic a bird into flushing instead of merely sneaking off without your ever knowing it.

■ Good places to hunt for ruffed grouse include old orchards, tangles of wild grapevines, alder runs, farm woodlots, hilly and juniper-grown pastures, forest edges and birch and evergreen pockets. Since they eat a wide variety of fruits, nuts, berries, seeds and insects, you may find game wherever there's a good concentration of any such food. Hence, they're unpredictable, but they do have a tendency to prefer high ground during the early season and lowlands later on as the weather gets cold. Unlike most upland birds, grouse do not "hold tight" for a pointing dog. On the contrary, they're notorious for wild flushes that permit little chance for a shot. Hunting them without a dog is a chancy endeavor (and far less fun), but that rarity known as a good grouse dog must work close to the gunner, never ranging out the way a quail dog does. For training purposes, a heavy chain or even a sash weight is sometimes fastened to the dog's collar to slow him down. Some hunters carry this principle still further by attaching a fifty-foot check cord to the collar. Theoretically, this is only for training, but it can be used on a fully trained dog if you're immune to the embarrassment caused by the remarks of other hunters. Probably the chief attribute of a good grouse dog is a nose so sharp that the animal freezes into a stanch point at a mere whiff of grouse before getting close enough to flush the bird.

■ Grouse and woodcock are often encountered in the same areas and are, of course, hunted together. The most likely woodcock spots are alder swales, young birch and poplar runs, brushy pastures—wherever the ground is apt to be rich in earthworms and soft enough for the birds to drill with their long bills. Although woodcock do eat other things, worms make up the bulk of their diet. Their presence can often be detected by the bored holes and the chalky spatter of droppings. Early in the season, most of the birds are likely to be "natives" rather than birds that have stopped for a while to rest and feed during their migration from the north. At this time, it's wise to hunt the lowlands, which are rich in food. But as the short migratory period progresses and the "flight birds" (migrants) arrive, woodcock begin to congregate on sunnier, warmer hillsides where birch and poplar patches provide good habitat. Unlike the grouse encountered in the same areas, they'll lie well for a dog, but when they do flush, their rise is a twisting, sudden ascent. In thick cover, you may have to shoot quickly, but they're easier to hit at the top of their rise if the treetops are sparse. When flushed in heavy cover, they usually fly toward the nearest opening, so that you can often position yourself for a good shot.

■ Bobwhite quail are covey birds, and a single big family of a dozen or up to twice that many, replenishing itself year after year, will be found in the same fields every season if the birds are not overgunned. They cluster to feed so that all the birds will be foraging over no more than, say, a sixty-foot spread until flushed and scattered. They like grains, soybeans, peas, weed seeds and berries. Just as they have favorite feeding and roosting spots, they have favorite escape covers, toward which they'll almost invariably fly. The covey only *appears* to explode in every direction. Having hunted a given covey a couple of times, a hunter knows the escape route and can approach so that the majority of the birds will fly straight away from him—offering relatively easy shots and the possibility of scoring a double on one flush. Never make the mistake of shooting into what looks like a cloud of quail; the cloud will disperse before your pattern reaches it, and you'll have little chance of hitting any of the birds. Pick one target quickly. A good pointing dog is vital in bobwhite hunting because this species of quail can lie perfectly still, perfectly camouflaged in a few inches of grass, and you might just step on a bobwhite without producing a flush. A dog is also essential for finding the singles after a flushed covey has scattered.

■ Scaled (or blue) quail like the arid country of the Southwest, and they are often hunted without a dog. However, they prefer running to flying and often run again when they alight. One of the best ways to put them up is to rush at them, and it helps to fire a shot. This generally causes them to flush, and you can then try a quick wing shot.

■ The same general areas, but lusher spots, are sometimes frequented by Gambel quail, and a dog is a help in hunting these birds. Particularly good covers are mesquite-choked places because these quail love mesquite beans. The best time to hunt is midday—if you can take the heat.

■ Doves of one species or another are found all over this country and are hunted in most states. The best whitewing shooting is in the Southwest and Far West, the best mourning-dove shooting in the Southeast. Flocks of mourning doves feed in open fields of corn, millet, rice, buckwheat, sorghum, peas or barley, and they also like sunflowers, croton and milo (a kind of sorghum). Since they tend to scout a field from a tree before coming in to feed, decoys propped in trees or at the banks of a watering spot will often bring them in. Another method is simply to conceal yourself near an isolated tree or at a field edge. Many hunters wear camouflage clothing. Pointing and flushing dogs are of no use, but it does pay to train a dog to retrieve doves. It also pays to scout an area by automobile and to ask local farmers and rural mail carriers where they've seen heavy concentrations of birds. The doves of the West and Southwest like the same general types of feed and habitat, but in less cultivated areas they can be found where there are wild grains and weed seeds. Pass shooting at doves is great practice for waterfowlers.

■ On big, open stubble or wheat fields, Hungarian partridge can be difficult to approach. They're especially wild flushers on wet, windy days. One good technique for getting shots is to cast your dog in a very wide circle, hoping to pin a covey between you and the dog until you get within range. Another method is to keep the dog nearly at heel and walk briskly, occasionally surprising a single or a covey.

■ Chukar partridge, unlike Hungarian partridge, prefer rugged terrain—even seemingly inhospitable canyons. Because they try to escape danger by running uphill, it's best to work canyons, slopes and draws from the top down. A startled covey will run, but a well-trained dog can circle ahead and flush them. They'll rise almost vertically for perhaps ten feet or more and then, like ptarmigan, streak downhill.

■ Turkeys may well be the most wary of all game birds and the most difficult to hunt, but certain characteristics make them vulnerable nevertheless. During the fall season, the toms roost alone or with a few other males, preferably in tall, thick pines, cypresses or cottonwoods. At dawn they may fly several miles to feeding spots rich in mast, fruits and berries. Because they are exceedingly fixed in their habits, they'll be found in just about the same spot at the same time, day after day, if they haven't been molested. Before the season opens, you can therefore scout for roosting trees and feeding areas. Then you can take a concealed stand before dawn, at a spot from which—if you remain absolutely quiet and stationary—you might ambush your Thanksgiving turkey. In areas that have a spring season, you can do some stalking, and you can take advantage of the mating instinct by luring the toms with a call. Look for sunny "strutting" areas, and be sure to master your call before you hunt. Turkeys are not easy to fool.

■ To attract dipper ducks—the shallow-water species—you don't need a big raft of decoys. A dozen will be quite enough for mallards, black ducks, pintail or teal, but they should be reasonably accurate imitations of the real birds. In areas where a number of species funnel through or linger during the southward migration, you can use just mallard blocks because most dippers will decoy to mallards. However, where there's a preponderance of the notoriously wary black ducks, it makes sense to use black-duck decoys.

■ Unless you're a traditionalist just for the sake of nostalgia, forget about the myth of having to use special decoy-placement patterns, such as the fish hook. Live ducks don't regiment themselves into fancy patterns on the water. More effective is a random-looking arrangement, as if the birds were paddling about and feeding. It's best to place the blocks several feet apart at least, both for good visibility from the air and for a natural appearance. The nearest decoys should be about twenty yards out from a blind that offers good concealment. Also bear in mind that all species of ducks tend to come in against the wind. If your decoys are in front of you and the breeze is coming from behind you as you sit in the blind, you will have an attractive setup. If the breeze is blowing from right to left, place your spread to the right so that the birds will come down directly in front of your blind. If it's blowing from the left, place the spread to the left.

■ To lure Canadas down over a stubble field or other likely feeding spot, you naturally use land decoys. Some of these blocks should have their necks arched downward in feeding position. A few can have their heads turned in a preening or resting attitude, but some—particularly one or two along the edge—should be in an alert, heads-up position because Canadas always seem to have sentinels watching out for the flock. When you are using a spread of land decoys (or pass shooting on land), a pit blind with a camouflaged top is best. Because Canadas have good vision, your head should be no higher than ground level unless standing cornstalks or other screening foliage will help conceal you. Another effective blind for this kind of shooting is a hedgerow on an edge of the field or standing cornstalks placed naturally along a row of corn.

■ Snow geese offer such a marked contrast to the intelligence of Canadas that one can understand the origin of the expression "silly goose." In the Texas rice fields and other snow-goose meccas, gunners don't bother with pit blinds or block decoys. The decoys are merely big white rags scattered on a field. The gunners, wearing white coveralls or draped in white bed sheets, lie down quietly among the rags, rising to shoot when the geese fly in close enough. Other species, such as specklebellies, will frequently accompany the snows, thus providing bonus shooting. Be sure you can recognize each breed in case one species has suffered a decline in number and is not currently legal to shoot.

■ Decoy spreads for diving species—the big-water ducks—differ from dipper-decoy spreads. Generally speaking, the scaup, or bluebill, is to divers as the mallard is to dippers; that is, a spread of scaup blocks will attract other species. But in areas where redheads and canvasbacks are plentiful, gunners may prefer imitations of these species or may use a decoy mixture. Since divers feed in large groups and in relatively deep water, the *best* spread is a big, rather compactly arranged "raft" of decoys—as many as fifty. A number of these should face in more or less the same direction, and they should be far out from shore.

■ You can occasionally manipulate the end of a decoy line to make the blocks bob naturally on the water. Some hunters even attach thin lines to a few of the decoy heads and run these lines through swivels on a main line to make the blocks tip up once in a while as if feeding.

■ You can protect your hands when setting out or picking up decoys by wearing rubber gloves. Instead of conventional rubber gloves, you may prefer trapper's gloves, which have extralong rubber gauntlets to keep your forearms dry.

■ Shiny decoys are a warning signal to birds. Paint them or touch them up with dull paint, flat rather than glossy. If a decoy looks shiny, dull it with sandpaper.

■ To fashion good homemade decoy anchors, you need nothing more than an old 150-watt light bulb, some plaster of paris, some lead and some heavy, rustproof wire. The plaster and wire are available at any hardware store. The lead, in the form of old tire weights, can be yours for the asking at a local garage. Mix the plaster in any small container, and use the light bulb—upside down—to press a convex depression into the middle of it. If you push the bulb about halfway in, then remove it, the "bowl" will be deep enough. This is your lead mold. Before pouring the molten lead into the mold, cut about a one-foot length of wire and bend it into the shape of the Greek letter *omega*—an inverted U with the ends bent outward. Pour the lead into the mold and then press the legs of the U into the lead. When it has cooled and hardened, remove it from the plaster. Attach the anchor line with a snap swivel, which is easily removable and prevents twisting, permitting the decoy to float naturally.

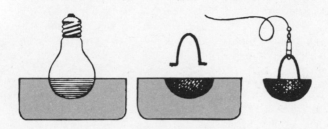

■ Jump shooting adds the excitement of upland-style flushing to the hunting of ducks. It works best along the banks of streams, small woods-ponds and potholes in marshlands and farmlands. There are two methods. One is to approach on foot, stealthily, preferably in a crouch. The other is to drift, pole or paddle very quietly down a waterway in a low-profile, camouflaged boat or canoe. Reed-colored paint is not sufficient camouflage for this. It's better to break up and mask the outline of the boat with reeds and grasses and/or tangled foliage and tree branches. A strip of inner tube tacked along the outer sides of the boat is a good holder for reed stalks. Just slip them, upright, between the strip and the gunwale. A camouflaged boat also makes a good mobile blind for pass shooting or decoying over water. You just maneuver the boat in among tall, concealing reeds and sit still. In such a situation, don't overdo the calling or you'll just scare off the birds. And practice your calling, matching it to a commercial duck-call phonograph record, because bad calling is far worse than none. Phonograph records are illegal for actual waterfowl hunting but are excellent for learning calls.

■ A temporary blind that can be set up and taken down very quickly can be made of ordinary old bamboo shades or curtains. Just unroll and prop up the bamboo shades, and then break up their outline with foliage.

■ Too many birds are crippled or missed by "sky busters," who shoot when the range is absurdly long. As a general rule, a duck is within excellent range—thirty to forty yards—when you can see its colors clearly. The green head of a mallard drake, and similarly distinctive features on some other species, may be seen at a slightly longer distance, and even a teal's little blue or green wing patch may be seen at forty yards if the light is good, but if you hold your fire until you can clearly distinguish such markings, you'll be a conservationist hunter. Novice hunters should hang birds of various types by the neck with wings extended, then step back about thirty or forty yards to determine what part of the bird is distinctly visible and use that as a future guide.

■ There are two other aids that can be employed to estimate waterfowl range. One is a stake driven in the ground forty or fifty yards from the blind. Use this as a range indicator and shoot at nothing until it has passed that stake. Sometimes a natural landmark will furnish a similar indicator. Another method is to use the front bead of your gun. If the bead entirely covers the head of a goose, the bird is not yet in range. Even with a duck, wait at least until the bead barely covers the head.

■ If you have no retrieving dog and you're hunting a pond or stream that's too deep for wading, take along a casting rod and a floating plug. You can cast out to fallen ducks, hook and retrieve them.

Gun Care Tips

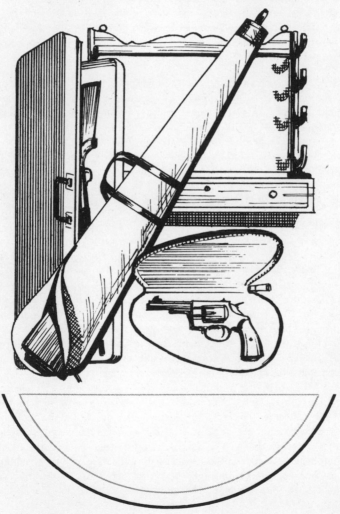

Gun care means more than just cleaning. It includes minor do-it-yourself repairs and the ego-shattering admission that *most* repairs should be left to the expert hands of a gunsmith or the manufacturer. It also includes employing certain storage techniques that will prevent rust or corrosion from setting in when a gun is put away for extended periods, plus a few little tricks to prevent damage in the field.

■ The action of any gun should be kept clean and lightly lubricated. Too much lubricant will attract dirt, causing moving parts to become sluggish and subject to wear and freeze-ups in extreme cold, but a very light film will reduce friction and protect against rust and corrosion.

■ Most American-made commercial primers for centerfires became nonmercuric and noncorrosive in the early 1930s, but there have been exceptions. Some military ammunition (particularly match cartridges) employed corrosive primers until about 1956, and some commercial match cartridges used them until 1960. It is therefore unwise to use old lots of commercial or military-surplus ammunition unless you know what kind of primer was used in the particular cartridges—or unless you clean your firearm with extra thoroughness immediately after every shooting session.

■ Although the notion is incorrect that a shotgun needs little or no attention because there's no rifling to snag particles and because some shotguns actually perform better after they've fired a few hundred shells, uninformed shooters believed that a coat of leading was good for a smoothbore. The improvement was *not* usually caused by "leading"—the adherence of lead rubbed off the pellets onto the bore surface—because this was likely to be streaky rather than uniform. Rather, it should have been attributed to the smoothing out of minuscule rough spots in the bore as pellets repeatedly rubbed the surface of the forcing cone (just ahead of the chamber), the bore proper and the choke.

Modern plastic shotgun shells employ a plastic wad column incorporating a shot cup, which not only minimizes deformation of the pellets as they're squeezed through bore and choke but also improves the pattern performance and protects the bore from leading. As wonderful as this is, you should still clean your shotgun periodically during the hunting season and after clay-target shooting. A quick glance through the barrel and into the receiver will make it obvious to anyone that powder residue and debris will have accumulated.

■ Particular care in cleaning should be taken after a waterfowl hunt on salt water because salt spray wreaks special havoc on metal and wood. In fact, any kind of hunt in a humid coastal area calls for a good posthunt cleaning to make sure no brine clings to the gun.

■ Always run your cleaning rod into the bore of a rifled arm from the breech unless the gun's design prevents this. In the case of bolt actions, the bolt should be removed for cleaning anyway, and doing so will give you access to the breech. Cleaning from the rear lessens the possibility of marring, nicking or wearing down the muzzle and thus impairing accuracy. Moreover, if you clean from the breech while keeping the muzzle pointed slightly downward, no dirty solvent or oil will drip back into the action. With the shotgun barrels, cleaning from the breech end is just as important, if at all possible, to ensure thorough cleaning of the chamber and to eliminate residue from the bore falling into the receiver. A dirty or rusted chamber in any firearm could cause extraction problems.

■ With a gun that can't be cleaned from the breech, take extra care as you insert the tip of the cleaning rod into the muzzle. You can guide it in with thumb and forefinger. You can also buy a commercial muzzle guard that works much like the detachable "false muzzles" on some antique target rifles. The modern version is a plastic plug with a hole in the center, which guides the rod in so that it doesn't touch the muzzle surface. It should not be left in the gun after cleaning—nor should any other barrel obstruction.

■ There are shooters who boast that they've never once cleaned a rimfire rifle or handgun. According to them, it has been unnecessary for almost fifty years—since the mid-1920s when Remington introduced the first American 22-caliber rimfire cartridges with noncorrosive, nonmercuric primers. Invented by a chemist named James E. Burns, the new primers replaced the mercury with lead styphnate sensitized by tetrazene. Some early primers of this kind eroded barrel steel, but soon the mixture was so well perfected that it actually had a protective effect when residue remained in an uncleaned bore.

And since 22 cartridges use unjacketed, lubricated lead bullets, rimfire shooters don't need to worry about tiny particles of centerfire bullet-jacket material stripping off and fouling the bore.

This sounds—and is—wonderful, but it doesn't alter the fact that neglect will eventually damage *any* firearm, including a 22. Although it isn't necessary to clean a rimfire barrel after every firing session or hunting day, it is advisable to give it a thorough cleaning every two or three months to keep it in top condition.

■ A gun should get an extra careful inspection several times a year —after a hunting trip, for example, and at the beginning and end of the season. Remove the magazine if it's a detachable box, and never take for granted that a tubular magazine is empty—make sure you see or feel the magazine plug. Examine the bore from both ends, as a small bit of foreign matter may be visible from one end but not from the other. Clean the bore with a solvent-soaked patch, then a dry patch, then hold the barrel up to the light and check again for any fouling. Easily removed parts should be cleaned with solvent as should the inside of the receiver and the magazine well. At this point, you're not finished cleaning the gun—you're just ready to begin the cleaning that you'd ordinarily give it.

■ A regular cleaning begins with the running of a solvent-soaked patch through the bore. But don't follow this immediately with a dry patch; leave the bore wet (to dissolve any residue) while you clean the exterior parts of the gun with the solvent. Then run a brush through the bore several times, followed by two or three more wet patches. Leave the barrel wet again while you clean the receiver and movable parts, first with solvent, then with dry patches or a cloth. By that time, anything left in the bore should have softened, and you can put a couple of dry patches through to complete the cleaning. Apply a very light film of oil inside and out, and the gun is ready to store away. But if you've done a lot of firing with it or haven't cleaned it in a long time, it may be advisable to leave solvent soaking in the bore overnight. If the barrel isn't detachable, stand the arm muzzle down on a piece of cloth, cardboard, rubber or other pad so that the dirty solvent won't leak back into the action. The cleaning can be finished the next day.

■ Even clean oil should not be allowed to run back onto moving parts because anything more than a thin protective film will collect gunk, possibly even causing an eventual malfunction. This is the reason that some gun racks and cabinets are designed to hold the muzzle lower than the receivers. It is even better to store guns vertically, with the muzzles down, so that no oil can seep from the receiver area back into the stock and cause wood deterioration and discoloration. Put a pad of rubber, cloth, plastic or other soft material under each muzzle, and prop the guns carefully so that they can't topple over. The storage enclosure should be securely locked.

■ Ammunition should be locked in a separate place, preferably cool and dry, not just to discourage theft but also to ensure the safety of inquisitive persons—particularly children—who may not know how to handle guns properly. Metal filing boxes or cabinets make good storage containers.

■ As a general rule, gun cases should be used only to carry and protect firearms in transit to and from the hunting area. If you store your guns in the cases, moisture may be trapped inside with them or may condense on them in damp weather. It will be slow to dry and will cause rusting. Cases lined with woolly sheepskin are the worst offenders. However, if absolutely necessary, guns that are properly cleaned and oiled could be stored in gun cases that are chemically treated with a good rust preventive. Most of the cases now available are already treated and have a padded rubber tip at the muzzle end. This will allow you to store your gun muzzle down. Do not leave guns cased or open in the trunk of a car. Overnight temperature and humidity change can be extreme in a trunk and rusting can occur overnight.

■ Chemically treated antirust disks or other dehumidifying, rust-preventive spray products can be purchased at most gun shops for treating the inside of your gun cases for additional gun protection.

■ Camphor is a passable substitute for commercial antirust products. You can put a chunk in your gun cabinet or a small piece in each case.

■ After handling a gun, wipe it with an oily cloth or with one of the commercial cleaning cloths that are impregnated with silicones or synthetic compounds. Tiny amounts of perspiration and skin oils, which are always present on your hands, will cause corrosion if not wiped off. The commercial cloths leave a very thin, invisible protective film on metal and wood.

■ If a gun is to be stored for a long period, a coating of gun grease will protect it better than thin oil but will be a nuisance to remove later. Never use fuel oil or anything else that might possibly cause corrosion.

■ A number of synthetic gun lubricants have recently been introduced. They are very effective in preventing rust and corrosion, and some gunsmiths prefer them to conventional gun oils.

■ Conventional oil thickens when the temperature drops; this can make the action of a firearm stick during cold weather just when you need to operate it quickly. Therefore, it is very important to use a gun oil that will not gum at low temperatures, or you can substitute powdered graphite for liquid lubricant. Both are available at gun stores, and they won't "freeze" a gun's action.

■ The color-corrected coating on the lenses of telescopic sights can be damaged and the glass itself can be marred if carelessly rubbed during cleaning. The best thing to use is a soft lens brush or a lens-cleaning cloth made for the purpose.

■ To remove a small light blotch of rust from a gun, soak it in solvent and then rub it with a typewriter eraser. If it's stubborn, rub it with a wad of fine steel wool with the solvent—but don't get over-eager or you may lighten the bluing or scratch the metal.

■ Paste and liquid preparations for touch-up bluing work well if you follow the manufacturer's instructions carefully, work on a small area of metal at a time and wipe the stuff off quickly. The longer it stays on, the darker the metal will get. The only way to match the surrounding bluing closely is with repeated applications, darkening the surface gradually.

■ A pipe cleaner is very handy for cleaning out the debris that gets caught in the little openings of a shotgun's ventilated rib.

■ A brass-wire brush is great for loosening up lead fouling and other stubborn debris in either a rifled or smoothbored barrel, but sometimes it won't do the trick even after the bore has had a soaking with solvent. In that case, buy a commercially available bore-cleaning compound at a gun shop, apply it sparingly on a patch and make several passes through the bore. Additional passes should be made in the bore ahead of the chamber because most fouling occurs in the first third of the barrel. Another method of removing bore fouling is the use of blue ointment, which can be purchased at your drugstore. Swab it generously into the barrel and let it stand for several hours. The mercury in the ointment will loosen the lead so that it can be brushed out. You may need to repeat the treatment if the barrel is badly leaded. Afterward, clean it thoroughly and oil it.

■ Before taking your gun out to shoot, run a dry patch through the bore. If there's much oil in the barrel, it can affect accuracy.

■ Rust in the bore can often be removed by commercial bore-cleaning compounds that can be purchased at most gun shops. Another method used is a half-and-half mixture of the finest valve-grinding compound and ordinary toothpaste. Apply the compound with a brass-wire cleaning brush and a swivel type cleaning rod so that the brush will follow the twist of the lands in a rifle or a handgun and give the bore a good scrubbing. After this treatment, use a conventional bore-cleaning solvent to get out all loosened matter and the cleaning mixture itself.

■ Muzzle-loading arms must be cleaned thoroughly and promptly after shooting. Very hot, soapy water and then a hot-water rinse should precede the solvent stage to remove the black-powder residue. Afterward, make sure all parts are thoroughly dried. Then clean and oil them in the normal manner.

■ When a handgun is to be left in a holster for a long period, rust can be deterred by saturating the leather with neat's-foot oil. Unlined leather cases for long arms may be treated the same way.

■ A dent can usually be removed from the stock of a shotgun or rifle by placing a damp cloth over the dented area and pressing it with a hot iron. This will raise the wood fibers that have been crushed inward. Some dents will require several such steamings, and spot refinishing of the stock will be necessary.

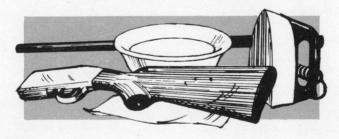

■ Home restocking of a shotgun is not recommended unless you have had considerable experience restocking rifles. The wood for many shotguns requires very difficult inletting and almost always requires delicate measuring and shaping to achieve a good fit.

■ If you yearn to try making a stock, remember that there's always the unfortunate possibility of botching the first job or, at best, failing to create a real work of art. You should therefore begin with a rifle that you don't care much about and buy a cheap stock blank. Plain black walnut is good stock material, relatively easy to work with and—in the lower grades—inexpensive. If no instruction sheet is furnished with the stock blank, ask the supplier for an instruction booklet.

■ Handgun grips (or, more properly, stocks) are far easier to make than rifle stocks, and blanks or rough-finished stocks are quite cheap. Checkering tools and instructions for using them are available through gun dealers and gunsmith-supply houses. Because neat, sharp checkering is difficult to do, you should practice on spare pieces of wood before attempting it on your finished stocks.

■ Iron sights that fit into dovetail slots in a gun barrel are always driven in from right to left, so they must be driven out from left to right. The slot is tapered for a tight fit, and a loose sight can be tightened by carefully tapping the edge with a small mallet.

■ Some handguns and rifles have interchangeable front sights, but if you have a gun whose sight is not removable, any alteration is likely to be a job for a gunsmith. However, if the trouble is just that the front sight doesn't show up well for woods hunting, a dab of red or white enamel will help remedy it. Or you can file its top to a forty-five-degree angle to catch more light.

■ An old toothbrush is handy for cleaning hard-to-reach or uneven surfaces on many guns. When dipped in solvent, it's particularly good for cleaning a revolver's extractor and ratchet.

■ The chambers of a revolver cylinder should be dry, not oily, when you load them. If the cartridges stick and are hard to extract, clean the chambers with a cotton swab dipped in lighter fluid.

■ It's considerably easier to refinish an old stock than to make a new one. First, however, it's necessary to take the stock off the gun. With most rifles this is easy, but with some shotguns it's complicated and may even require an assortment of special screwdrivers and other tools that you don't have. It's best, therefore, to have your gunsmith remove such a stock for you and put it back on after you've refinished it. His charge will be nominal.

■ The first step in refinishing a stock is to take off the old finish. Coat the wood heavily with paint-and-varnish remover, working on one small area at a time so that the stuff won't dry out, and scrape it away with a dull knife. After repeating this several times, you'll have most of the finish off and you can smooth the rest away with fine-grit sandpaper. Leave any checkered areas alone unless you have the special tools, skill and desire to rechecker the wood. Once it has been sanded smooth, wet it down with a damp rag and then use heat to dry it quickly. This will raise the "fur" on the wood. Rub off the small raised particles with steel wool. Repeat this until the wetting-drying operation raises virtually no more particles or fibers. Several brands of oil finishes are available at gun shops. The finish is also a sealer, but some craftsmen prefer to ensure complete sealing before finishing by applying a thin coat of shellac or bar-top varnish, letting it dry for forty-eight hours, and repeating. There are also commercial fillers that can be used for protection against warping, swelling or discoloration; applied according to the manufacturer's directions, a filler can reduce the number of oil coats needed for a good finish. Commercial oil finish has an additive to hasten the drying time for each application. Apply it by hand-spreading and rubbing a few drops at a time over the entire stock, allowing several hours' drying time between coats. Depending on how deep a tone you want, you'll probably apply several coats. At the same time, apply the finish under the butt plate and other interior stock surfaces to completely weatherproof the stock. Each coat except the last is sanded with fine-grit paper to fill the wood pores. Apply a final coat in the same way as previous coats, using as little oil as possible for a smooth, high-sheen finish. Should you desire to have a soft sheen, tone the finish down by using 000 steel wool. When you've completed the job, examine it to decide whether it needs still another coat. It will probably look handsome as is, and you can always add coats at the end of future hunting seasons.

■ If you can't pack a complete cleaning kit for a hunting or fishing trip, at least take along a small squeeze can of gun oil, a few patches, a silicone cleaning cloth and a length of string longer than the gun's barrel. Drop the string into the breech end so that it hangs out of the muzzle. Then tie a patch onto the free end of the string at the breech and pull it through to clean the bore. No cleaning rod is more collapsible and compact than this, but there are commercial rods that actually can be coiled for packing or carrying and then straightened out and, by a simple twist, locked for cleaning.

Bow Hunting and Archery

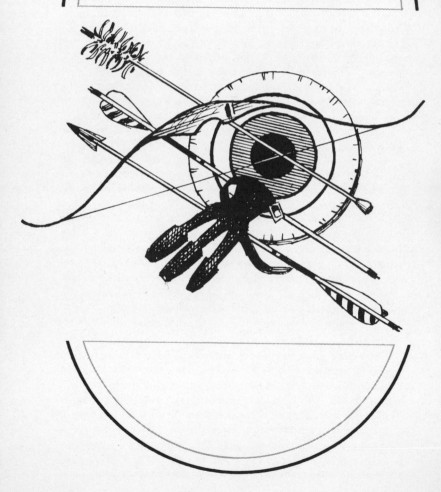

As with air guns, skill with the bow may be developed even in densely populated areas through plinking and target practice. Of course, adequate backstops must be employed for safety's sake. Field archery is a target game that simulates actual hunting conditions with a wide variety of target sizes and shooting distances. It is fun in itself and excellent training for archery hunting. Field archery clubs maintain many ranges and welcome new members and guests.

■ At most times during the hunting season, a tree stand (where legal) will just about double your chances for scoring on deer. Tree stands can be elaborate permanent affairs or simply the tree you happen to choose in a promising area. Of course many times trees may not offer climbing possibilities. To prepare yourself for this eventuality, pack in a small fold-up ladder to your stand. Some bow hunters make their own from tubular aluminum or wood. These are two- or three-step devices with an L bend at the top over which is attached a small platform. The top of the ladder is leaned against the tree trunk and strapped in place. The hunter perches on the platform and waits—in a position he can comfortably hold for a long time. In fairly thick woods you don't have to be high. Some stands are rigged as low as six-and-a-half feet.

■ A handful of straw or long grass picked at the hunting grounds can be bent into a U shape and stuffed loosely into a quiver top (with the bottom of the U downward) to prevent arrows from rattling and spooking game. The material comes off easily should a hunting point catch in it.

■ Bowmen hunting carp and other "rough" fish in the spring, when the fish come into the shallows to breed, should concentrate their efforts during the mornings and evenings. The wind tends to be at calm at these times, permitting easy spotting of the fish. Remember to aim below the point from which you see the fish to correct for refraction. Water "bends" light, making the fish appear to be above the level it actually is when viewed from an angle.

■ A general rule for bow hunters, which many experts swear by, is to take a stand when hunting whitetail but to move for mule deer. Mulies at times, primarily when they're on the move, will tolerate a considerable amount of noise without spooking—noise that would send the typical whitetail into the next county.

■ There are certain conditions under which you can still-hunt (a slow-paced stop-and-go hunting tactic) for whitetail, elk or other easily spooked game. Try it when leaves are wet from rain or in areas where you don't have to worry about leaf rustle. When light powdery snow covers the ground, this method works very well.

■ You should wear camouflage when you hunt with a bow but it doesn't have to be the kind especially made for archers or waterfowlers. Except for the net material, most camouflage cloth is rough and noisy in the brush. During cold weather, plaid patterns in wool will provide excellent camouflage as far as animals are concerned. For warmer weather, consider a soft shirt in muted tones with a fairly good-sized pattern. Just avoid solid colors because the objective is to break up your silhouette.

■ When hunting varmints with a bow, choose terrain that is a bit heavier with vegetation than that which a rifleman would select. This permits closer shooting. A disadvantage to varmint hunting in such close quarters, however, is that the animal will appear suddenly—probably from an unexpected quarter—and will be gone again unless you are constantly alert. Woodchuck hunting is growing rapidly in popularity. It requires the height of perfection in the art of stalking.

■ The thirty-yard mark seems to be the nemesis of many deer hunters. At that range, a deer can easily move five feet from his original position by the time a fired arrow closes in. The animal takes off fast when startled by the bowstring twang. At closer range he *usually* doesn't react in time, and at more distant ranges, the noise is not as ominous. Best advice is to use a bowstring silencer. You can make one by simply slipping two small lengths of broad rubber band between the braids of the bowstring near both ends of the bow, or you can purchase some of the ready-made silencers at an archery tackle shop. The noise of drawing an arrow can easily spook a deer. A piece of chamois or soft leather glued in the sight window of the bow will silence the arrow against the bow.

■ Especially on rough terrain, an arrow should not be carried in the nocked position while still-hunting. When a hunter is moving along with nocked arrow pointed down, all it takes is a slight stumble to drive the hunting head through the top of his leather boot. Each hunter must develop his own favorite carry for the first-shot arrow. Some bowmen carry it loose in the same hand that grips the bow. Others prefer a quick-release quiver of the kind that attaches to the bow.

■ When using a ground blind, cut two forked branches, each about one-and-a-half feet long. Sharpen and drive the unforked ends into the ground a couple of feet apart in front of your sitting position. You can then rest your bow horizontally in the forks, with an arrow nocked and ready to go. Picking up the bow from this position is easy and silent.

■ Just as an elevated blind is generally more effective than one on the deer's level, a surface blind can be improved by digging a two-foot-deep hole in which to place your legs. More of your bulk is then below the animal's normal alert level, and the blind walls need only be a short height above ground.

■ Once you've constructed a blind, it's a good idea to take a few practice shots from it in different directions. This will give you a chance to detect and remove any twigs or branches that could deflect an arrow.

■ When bow fishing for fish expected to be over five pounds, use a solid fiberglass arrow. Hollow glass or wood can break if a fish rolls, and aluminum shafts are too light. The heavier solid arrow also penetrates more water with greater effect. Also, use rubber fletching on a fishing arrow. Otherwise you'll spend time straightening out water-matted feathers.

■ When hunting for really big fish such as sharks, rays or alligator gar, forget the usual spool arrangement normally fastened to the bow. Instead, pull fifteen or twenty yards of line from a big-game reel on a fishing rod. Fasten the line to the harpoon arrow, place the coils in a bucket or fly fisher's line-stripping basket attached around your waist. Then, when you hit, you can put down the bow and battle the monster with a rod and reel.

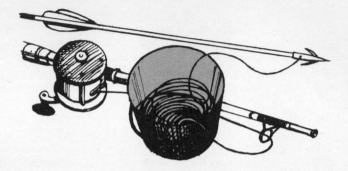

■ Always keep broadheads covered in the field or at camp. Bow quivers should be hooded, not only to protect the hunting heads but to eliminate the possibility of a nasty accident.

■ When hunting in rainy or snowy weather, tie a small plastic bag around your feathers with string or a rubber band. This keeps them from becoming matted, which affects flight characteristics. A quick tug will pull the bag loose when you need to shoot.

■ When attaching sights, never put screws into the bow where it bends. Use a strong tape, such as packing tape. It will do the job just as well and leave no ugly scars if you decide to remove the sight.

■ Soiled and matted fletching can be restored by the same method fly fishermen use to rejuvenate hackles on dry flies. Simply hold the feathers over a spout of steam from a teakettle or pot for a few seconds.

■ Broadheads, once sharpened, should be coated with grease or oil to keep them from rusting. And while on the subject of sharpening, never file a hunting head to a long, thin point. A tip should be dubbed off or rounded to a chisel point. The slender, extreme point will only curl when striking hard bone.

■ Arrows rubbed with wax or paraffin penetrate more easily when you are hunting, and they also pull out more easily from bales of hay or other targets and backstops when you practice.

■ Sawtooth edges on broadheads, although they look ferocious, are to be avoided. The teeth clog with hair and tissue, impeding penetration.

■ In the days of all-wood bows, hunters thought in terms of sixty-five- to seventy-five-pound draw weight. Today's laminated bows are so effective that it takes less draw weight to get the job done. Nevertheless, the average beginning hunter must work to build up the ability to handle a bow heavy enough to take big game. About forty-five pounds of draw weight should be considered for deer. A thirty-five pounder can do the job and is much preferred by women and younger shooters, but if they can use a heavier weight so much the better. A fifty-five- or sixty-pound bow should be considered the minimum for big game like elk or moose. In choosing the first bow, never overburden yourself. It is best to start with an inexpensive, light weapon and then move up when you're ready. If pulling the bow is a strain at first and you can shoot only half a dozen times at one session without getting shaky, then stop—shoot only as many times as you can with correct form. After that, rest—possibly without touching the bow again that day. Keep practicing regularly, however, and in very short order your muscles will be strong enough to handle the bow with ease. If you are not familiar with archery, seek the advice of an expert in selecting and fitting a bow to you and your needs and matching it with the proper arrows.

■ Match the spine (stiffness) of the arrow to the bow. Arrows that are too stiff will cast to the left of aiming point for a right-hander. Arrows that are too soft will cast right or they may break—and a broken shaft may deflect into the shooter's bow hand.

■ Broadhead arrows must be long enough that the sharp head is not drawn back into the bow hand—generally, they should be about two inches longer than target or field-point arrows.

■ Learn proper technique for bracing (stringing) the bow to avoid twisting the limbs—the most common cause of bow damage. Use a stringing device; they are inexpensive and readily available.

Conservation

Most outdoors enthusiasts today are gaining a new awareness of how even their smallest actions can affect the environment. It has become the rule rather than the exception to carry a waste container in car, camper, boat or snowmobile and to dispose of waste at approved locations. Picnickers, too, carry refuse bags and clean up picnic areas before leaving. Holding tanks are no longer being emptied haphazardly—or furtively—by many people, and no one seems to mind waiting his turn at a dumping station. Campers are being careful to extinguish their fires completely, saturating the ashes with water and covering them with soil, and are generally leaving campsites cleaner than they were when they arrived.

■ Next time you're on a favorite fishing stream or lakeshore, stick an occasional willow shoot into the ground along the banks as you move on. These take root easily, help prevent erosion and provide needed shade and cover for fish. A project requiring a bit more energy is the shoreline planting of shrubs or other plants indigenous to the area.

■ When you prune the shrubs or trees in your yard, don't burn the prunings. Take them to the woods or unused fields and make piles of them. Such brush piles provide cover for small game and birds. Eventually brush will decay, thereby enriching the soil. Some prunings are beneficial in another way—they can provide winter feed for certain species. The best time to prune wild or run-down apple trees is when the snow is deep. The dropped branches will furnish winter feed for deer and rabbits as well as cover for small game.

■ No sportsman wants to believe that his own dog would run deer, but the observations of conservation officials indicate that almost any dog may be guilty of this at one time or another. Hunting with your dog is one thing; allowing the animal to roam the woods unaccompanied is another. Your dog should not be permitted to wander off your property. Neither should your domestic cat be permitted to run free, since it will prey on small game and birds.

■ A small fish that you intend to release will have a better chance for survival if you avoid handling it. The best way to release it is to slide your hand down the leader to the fish and then bend the fly or lure back and forth to free the hooks. If the fish is completely exhausted, cup one hand beneath its belly to steady it until it can navigate under its own steam. You can also rock such a fish gently from side to side to start aerated water working through its gills.

■ Nothing is more appalling than the sight of a whitetailed deer killed by a stray dog or pack of dogs. If you find such a carcass, or if you spot stray dogs or signs of strays in the woods, notify your local wildlife department immediately so that a conservation officer can round up these no-longer-domestic predators. In some areas, packs of wild dogs have actually endangered human beings.

■ While hunting or checking fencerows, you may find old posts scattered along the ground. If you arrange some of them into small, loose piles, they will form spots of cover for small game and birds, such as quail. Without further attention, each of these cover spots will gradually improve as vegetation grows around and through it.

■ Monofilament makes excellent fishline, but broken-off lengths of it can be deadly to all forms of life—including man. With or without hooks attached, mono has been responsible for entangling waterfowl and various water-oriented mammals. It has even been a hazard to skin divers on offshore wrecks. Next time you dredge up a "bird's nest" of the stuff, keep the lure you may find at one end, but wad up the mat of line and fasten it together with tape or pipe cleaner. In this fashion you can easily pocket the mess and take it home to be properly disposed of.

■ When putting out ears of corn for wildlife, impale them on sticks about six inches above the ground or snow. Birds and rabbits can then reach them but mice can't, and the feed will be less likely to be buried by new snow.

■ Farmers rage when woodchuck holes become too numerous, but the burrows are beneficial to other wildlife, particularly cottontail rabbits. The rabbits seek the protection and insulation of vacated dens in very cold weather. Do not destroy or fill in the burrows in any location in which they do not interfere with farming. Leave them alone—or, better yet, cover them with a loose screen of brush, held in place by a stone or small log. Rabbits will be able to get through a sufficiently loose screen (just think of the way they can penetrate brambles when you hunt them), but dogs and other large predators will be blocked.

■ Planting shrubs along irrigation ditches will deter erosion while providing cover and feed for wildlife. Their shade will help to minimize loss of water to evaporation.

■ Prescribed burning-off of certain fields and even woodlots can help both plant and animal life. Ask your state forestry department or county agricultural agent whether such a prescribed burn may be legal and advisable on some part of your property. Be sure to have adequate firebreaks and fire-stopping equipment ready, and do the burning under the supervision of a forestry agent or other qualified professional. In many areas, a permit is required for this project. Because of the hazards involved, first check with local authorities.

■ If you live near abandoned farmland and are willing to buy "wildlife seedlings" from either a commercial game farm or a conservation agency, you may be able to establish new game in your area. In some regions, for example, wild turkey poults will thrive where open woods are impinging on old farms. Other regions may be suitable for anything from quail to chukar to doves. Projects of this sort sometimes involve too much time, effort and money for an individual but may be an ideal undertaking for a group or club. Consult your state conservation department about appropriate species and methods of release. Remember, however, that openings are as important as cover plants in meeting the needs of wildlife. And maintaining openings may be as important as planting. Check with your conservation department.

■ Apple trees on abandoned land that is reverting to forest often fail to produce fruit because of crowding by other maturing timber. By cutting down the competing trees around these old apple trees, abundant autumn food is created for deer, grouse, bears and other wildlife.

■ In the top six to eight inches of soil, nature has perfected an excellent biological disposal system that works to decompose organic waste. Keep this in mind while preparing sanitary facilities on backpacking treks in the wilderness. "Catholes" should be no deeper than eight inches and at least fifty feet from any open water. Try to keep the sod intact. After using, fill the holes with soil and tramp it down. Nature will take care of the rest in a few days.

■ Burying cans and other food receptacles is no longer acceptable in an age of increasing utilization of wild lands. Paper materials may be burned. Cans too should be burned to eliminate food residue, then flattened and toted with you, leaving nothing for animals to uncover and strew about later. If food containers aren't too heavy or bulky to carry to your campsite, the empties certainly are easy enough to carry out.

■ Animals seek the cover of brush or hedgerows along field edges, where they can gain both food and protection. Edging fields with a shrub, such as multiflora rose, can benefit such species as quail, pheasant and rabbit. If you want to plant a strip of something that will taste as good to you as to the cottontails, raspberries are a good bet. Rabbits also like sumac bark, which has a high fat content that nourishes them when deep snow makes foraging difficult. In addition to hedgerows between fields and woods, the windbreaks on many farms offer usable habitat—oases of cover that make good feeding stations for birds.

■ Carbon—which is what your campfire remainders are made of—is not known for its degradability. When one camping party after another builds up and spreads out the pile, it can harm fragile vegetation, ultimately causing erosion. Instead of leaving charcoal, partly burned stumps, log ends, etc., for the next party to build a fire upon, crush them as much as possible and bury them. Burial—after soaking with water—also helps to ensure that a fire is really out. If the fire is completely cold, it is permissible to scatter a few of the pieces, as long as they don't create an eyesore.

■ During quail season, persuade all the members of your rod and gun club—or all your hunting friends—to carry afield little containers filled with bicolor lespedeza seed. Empty medicine bottles or plastic bags are fine for the purpose. Every once in a while during a hunt, make a little kick-spot in the ground with your boot heel and sprinkle seed into it. This will quickly increase the food supply and keep coveys in the area for future seasons.

■ Another good game-food plant is crown vetch, which is eaten by deer and used as cover by many kinds of wildlife. Landowners will do well to plant it in a fallow field or strip of land that isn't being otherwise utilized. It will continue to grow for years and is even good for the land, putting enough nitrogen into the soil that fertilizer isn't needed. If corn has been previously planted in the same field, it can be left as additional feed. More ambitious planters may want to put in a mixed crop of corn and crown vetch in otherwise unused spots. Planted on slopes, crown vetch is an excellent aid in erosion control as well.

■ Another good way to use an undeveloped piece of land is to put in a duck and trout pond. First check with your county agent and the forestry and conservation departments. You will get free advice on how and where to build the pond, what plantings will bring wildlife to it and where to buy the plantings cheaply. In some states, you can even get financial assistance for this kind of project.

■ Although some of the new self-styled conservationists have taken a hands-off-everything stand concerning the environment, the practices of harvesting, clearing, thinning and planting are imperative to the survival of animals, vegetation, fish and unpolluted water as nonurban habitat shrinks. Consult a local forester or the conservation department about any land you own or nearby land where it is permissible to make improvements. You may be advised to prune certain stunted, unhealthy or crowded lower tree branches to permit better growth of timber. You may even be advised to weed out some species of tree that is certain to die in a given location or is overabundant and crowding out other vegetation. A so-called mature woods is inevitably a dying woods, and proper weeding induces second growth needed by all sorts of wildlife, from grouse to deer. Remember, too, that large dead trees, especially those with cavities, are important to the survival of many species—wood ducks, squirrels, woodpeckers and other hole nesters. Because diversity in cover types is the key to wildlife improvement, the intent of the forestry operation should be made clear to the consulting forester.

■ Sportsmen often fish rivers, ponds and streams in the same marsh areas where they will be hunting waterfowl when the season opens. Wild rice, which provides feed not only for waterfowl but for countless other types of birds, will prosper in many such places. Keep a sack of wild-rice seed in your tackle box, and occasionally toss some out along marshy shorelines. A satisfying percentage will germinate and grow well in places where soil and water movement combine to provide suitable growing conditions.

■ In places where even willow shoots won't take root, sustain stream banks with a riprap of stones and rocks to slow down erosion and siltation. Severe siltation covers food and eggs and sometimes clogs fish gills.

■ Jetties, breakwaters, spillways, V dams and weirs all serve specific functions in streams. They divert flows, provide natural holding places for fish, create collecting areas for fish food, carve pools and raise the oxygen content of the water. They are often simple to build, providing excellent projects for families or clubs. A state fish or wildlife biologist can supply you with the know-how and tell you where such structures will be beneficial as well as where they might be useless or even harmful. In some states, however, it is illegal to undertake private stream improvement projects; check first with your state fisheries division.

■ One valuable fish-aid project can be carried out at the same time that you're prospecting trout waters. As most anglers know, a very likely holding spot for trout is in the bulge of current above a big rock on a long, fairly shallow flat—or along either side of the rock or in the hole that forms behind it. Without this kind of holding spot, the same shallow flat may remain sterile. When you find such a spot, roll a boulder out into the middle of the water. But even in a wide stream, give careful thought to its placement. If the boulder is too close to the bank, it can deflect the current and sections of the bank may be washed away during the spring run-off period of high, fast water. Moreover, if the current is sluggish or the space too narrow, the boulder may form a debris-gathering dam that will check the flow.

■ Plant annual food plots to provide feed for birds and game animals. Corn, millet, wheat, lespedeza, sunflowers and sorghum are prime examples of food plants used by many species. Plant woody cover crops adapted to local conditions; sow food shrubs

such as autumn olive, Tartarian honeysuckle and dogwood. Results of the latter are not as immediately evident as those of the grain-food plots, but in a few years you will have wildlife cover and food that will last for a long time. Consult your local wildlife manager or soil conservationist to ensure your using plants that are adapted to your area.

■ In quail country, anyone who raises chickens can increase the bobwhite population. Build three- by five-foot baskets out of two-inch-mesh poultry wire. In each basket place a wooden box, such as an apple crate, and put straw or other bedding material in the crate, together with a poultry feeder and water. Add a setting hen and a dozen quail eggs (obtained from a commercial source or the wildlife department). Place this setup next to a field of good feed and cover. The chicks can go through the wire, feeding outside during the day. They'll return to the warmth and safety of the hen at night but will grow up as wild as "native" birds and will have a better survival rate than pen-raised quail.

■ Puddle ducks, such as the mallard, can be encouraged to nest in boxes placed four to five feet off the ground, provided that some incubator-hatched hens are present in a new area to kick things off. There are many types of boxes. Some are manufactured, some come in kit form. You can also build your own. Metal or wood boxes should have a nest space of about fourteen by twelve by ten inches and should be equipped with predator guards. These guards are inverted funnels placed around the support poles beneath the boxes and pointed or highly slanted roofs. The enclosed nesting portion should be well below the access hole so that the eggs will not be visible to crows or owls.

Query your local fish and wildlife department to learn whether areas near your home are suitable for bird breeding.

Index

189

Additional copies of this Outdoor Tips book
can be obtained by sending $2.95 to

Outdoor Tips
P.O. Box 731
Bridgeport, Connecticut 06601

I enclose $ _____ for _____ copies of the book.

NAME _____

ADDRESS _____

CITY _____ STATE _____ ZIP _____

Additional copies of this Outdoor Tips book
can be obtained by sending $2.95 to

Outdoor Tips
P.O. Box 731
Bridgeport, Connecticut 06601

I enclose $ _____ for _____ copies of the book.

NAME _____

ADDRESS _____

CITY _____ STATE _____ ZIP _____

Additional copies of this Outdoor Tips book
can be obtained by sending $2.95 to

Outdoor Tips
P.O. Box 731
Bridgeport, Connecticut 06601

I enclose $ _____ for _____ copies of the book.

NAME _____

ADDRESS _____

CITY _____ STATE _____ ZIP _____